Everything About Guitar Chords

SEVENTH EDITION

By Wilbur M. Savidge

Exclusive Publication Rights:
PRAXIS MUSIC PUBLICATIONS, INC.

ISBN 1-884848-00-1

This book, like so many things in life, would not have been possible without the encouragement of my many friends, students and acquaintances through the years.

To each and every one — a warm THANK YOU!

CREDITS:
Cover Photography - Catalog Productions, Inc.
Cover design - Eddie Stafford
Book design - Wilbur Savidge
Production - Wilbur Savidge
Printing - Vicks Lithograph & Printing Corporation

Cover Guitar:
Martin D-35 P
Courtesy - Craig's Music, Weatherford, Texas

A PRODUCT OF PRAXIS MUSIC PUBLICATIONS, INC.
Bedford, Texas

A WORD FROM THE AUTHOR

This book was written over a five-year period of time—a time when I supported my family entirely from teaching the guitar, so I feel qualified to offer the following comments.

There is a need for better education material for the guitar student and teacher. Most books are written for those with little understanding of the guitar, or so complex that only a genius can understand them. Since most of us fall somewhere in-between, the following comment (and I hear it quite frequently from prospective buyers of books) is all too true: *"If you can understand the book, you don't need it, and if you need help you won't find it in any book."*

I have taught half hour private lessons and one hour class lessons with students as young as six to the older adult, and through the years I have found that there is a way of teaching music properly on the guitar. The underlying theme of proper teaching is the same for the guitar as in any field of learning. However, unlike piano, many guitar books are merely an expression of the author's abilities as a player and little if any programmed procedure is followed which utilizes all avenues of modern teaching concepts.

I, like most amateur guitarists, have little natural ability, learning has been quite difficult. If I have succeeded it is because: If I can understand it, it has to be logical and if I can understand it, I can teach it. It is not enough, I believe, to say two plus two equals four. We teachers must help the student understand how to add, subtract, multiply and divide. Statements are not enough. Nothing should be left to speculation. If a book is to provide help, then everything should be clearly explained and each musical concept taught in logical order.

I hope this book will prove to be a good example. While I'm sure there will be need for future revision, I believe the material, its sequence of presentation, design and special art work will aid you in your study of the guitar.

Bill Savidge

2

HOW TO USE THIS BOOK

This book covers—HOW TO PLAY GUITAR, BASIC THEORY, BASIC CHORDS, BARRE CHORDS, ADVANCED THEORY, AND JAZZ CHORDS.

Each page, starting with page five is a step by step logical sequence of knowledge. You will be led through every phase of chord theory, chord fingerings and positions, providing you with a working textbook of this complex subject.

Each pair of pages covers a single idea, and is complete in itself. No terminology will appear that has not been already explained on preceding pages.

CROSS REFERENCE—If you do not understand some term or concept, go to the cross reference index at the end of the book and look up the page where the subject is completely explained.

Better yet, if you feel you are weak on theory (why things work), start with Basic Chord Theory and read the entire book at least one time.

BASIC CHORD CHART—On pages 72 and 73 we have a chord chart showing the more common fingerings for seven type chords of each alphabetical name—*A*, *B*, *C*, *D*, etc. This will aid you in learning to play the simpler chords. For example: If you need to learn *Cdim*, look under *C* chords and you will find *Cdim*. This section of the book is actually a basic chord book.

CHORDS BY KEYS—Pages 76 through 83 present basic chords by KEY grouping. This is the only way chords are usable. If you are going to play in the key of *G*, page 83 will show the three primary chords and two minor chords that are most commonly used to play rhythm in this key.

FORMULAS FOR BUILDING CHORDS—On page 60 we present 20 chord formulas for building most of the more commonly used chords. This page will show you how to determine the notes that form each chord.

TRANSPOSING—Page 60 is useful also if you want to change a song from one key to another (transposing). By utilizing the information on this page you determine chords for most any new key.

CONTENTS

HOW TO PLAY GUITAR

KNOW YOUR GUITAR

To play the guitar we must first find out what the guitar is and how it works. Study the pictures and learn the names of the parts that make up the guitar. Become an expert on the various parts of the guitar.

Do you know where the HEAD is?

Do you know where the NUT is?

Do you know where the BRIDGE is?

WHAT YOU MUST DO TO PLAY THE GUITAR

The guitar is fun, easy to play and offers a new challenge every week. Being told what to do will not make you a good guitarist; these four things you must do.

OWN A REASONABLY GOOD GUITAR.

HAVE THE DESIRE TO LEARN TO PLAY IT.

OBTAIN THE KNOWLEDGE NECESSARY TO PLAY WELL.

PRACTICE, PRACTICE, PRACTICE.

Remember — you Must have the desire to play. You Must know what to do, and you Must practice. Without doing these four things you will never learn to play the guitar.

KNOW YOUR GUITAR

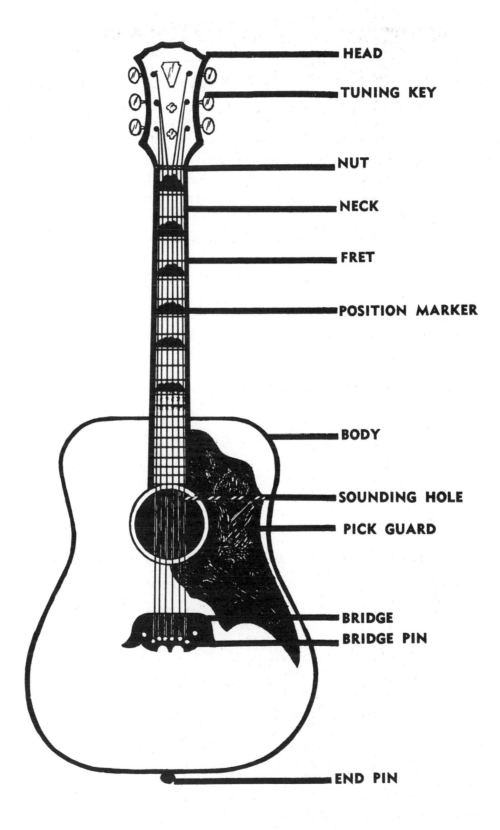

HEAD

TUNING KEY

NUT

NECK

FRET

POSITION MARKER

BODY

SOUNDING HOLE

PICK GUARD

BRIDGE
BRIDGE PIN

END PIN

HOW TO PLAY GUITAR

TUNING THE GUITAR

Guitar music is a series of pleasant tones when played properly. If the guitar is out of tune, no one can play it. Have you ever played a record at the wrong speed? It doesn't sound good, and a guitar out of tune won't either.

Listen to the instructor, listen to the guitar. Train your ears to what a properly tuned guitar sounds like.

The diagrams on the following page show us how to tune the guitar to itself. Be sure you understand how this is done.

Turn the tuning key for the low E string (6th string) till the string will ring without buzzing on the frets. Do not tune it too high.

Then place your finger on the sixth string at the fifth fret. Pick the string and tune the open fifth string till the two tones match. Follow the diagrams and tune each of the other strings the same way. While it is not necessary, we recommend you purchase a good guitar pitch pipe, and learn to use it. Remember, don't hesitate to ask the instructor for assistance should you need it.

HOLDING THE GUITAR

The guitar should be held almost vertically in a comfortable position. It will be necessary at first to tilt the bottom out so you can see the fingerboard, but don't let it lay flat. The further you lay the guitar over, the harder it is to place your fingers around the neck.

Keep the Head of the guitar high, don't point it at the floor. The guitar should be held vertically with the head close to the shoulder.

PICK ANGLE

The pick should slide down across the strings. Observe the angle of the pick in relation to the strings in the picture on the following page.

Hold the pick as shown and "Gently" strum the strings. Remember how the instructor does it. You do NOT want a hard stroke. You do not have to beat the guitar to make a pleasant sound. Hold the pick loosely, and use a gentle stroking action. Playing loud does not make you play better.

STRUMMING THE GUITAR

Sounds are made on the guitar by striking the strings, causing them to vibrate. There are several ways of doing this. Some guitarists use their fingers, and some use a thumb pick. However, the most commonly used method is the "Flat Pick." We recommend it, and the pictures in this book show the proper usage of the "Flat Pick."

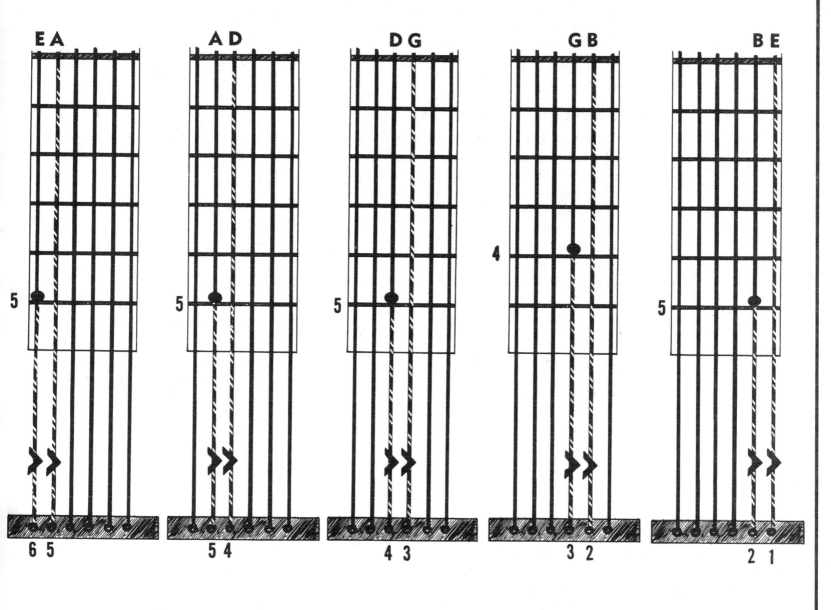

STRUMMING THE GUITAR

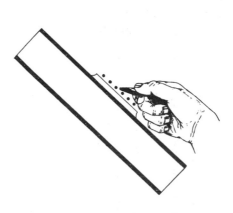

HOLDING THE GUITAR

PICK ANGLE

USING THE LEFT HAND

Improper placement of the palm and thumb is a common fault of all beginners. Use the thumb for support and KEEP the palm away from the neck. If the guitar is setting properly, you should not need to hold the neck up. When the palm is against the neck it becomes difficult to finger the strings properly. When pressing a string down, place the finger just behind the fret, not on it, or too far behind it. Take your time and learn each thing well. Remember, the things that seem hard, and often impossible today, will be easy tomorrow. Don't become discouraged.

FINGER NAILS

To play the guitar we use the ends of our fingers. You MUST keep your fingernails clipped short.

CALLOUSES

It is very difficult for beginning students to press the string down and obtain a clear sound while the string is plucked. This problem is caused by two things. Poor guitar necks, where the strings are abnormally high, and soft fingers. Press a string down and observe the end of your finger. The string leaves a depression. Callouses will prevent this and will make fingering easier. You will have sore fingers at first; however, callouses will develop quickly, if you keep practicing.

LEFT HAND TECHNIQUE

KEEP THE PALM AWAY FROM NECK

FRETTING STRING PROPERLY

KEEP FINGERS OVER TOP OF NECK

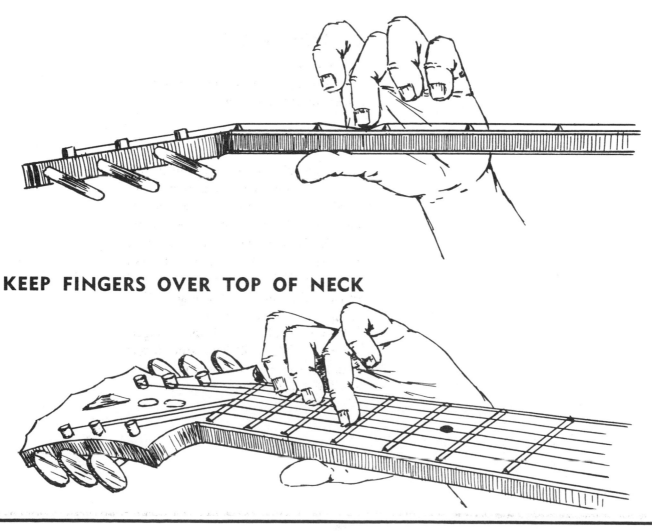

READING THE TIME SIGNATURE

Music is written on a STAFF. The staff has five horizontal lines, and is divided into measures by a BAR, a heavy vertical black line.

We have already learned that music is written in given keys (pitch), and a given rhythm (beat). The TIME SIGNATURE tells us this necessary information. At the beginning of each song, on the first staff, we will find the TREBLE CLEF. Directly after the clef, are numbers arranged above one another, and this is called the TIME SIGNATURE. These numbers tell us how the music is divided up. The top number tells us how many beats, or counts there are in each measure. The bottom number refers to note values, which we will learn later. For now we want to know how many beats there are to each measure, so we can play the rhythm properly.

RHYTHM — COUNTING TIME

Music can be said to be a science of timing and rhythm. You can not play the guitar if you do not develop a keen sense of these two important aspects of music. Playing alone, or with a group, you do not sound good if you do not have rhythm and timing.

You have seen musicians keeping time by tapping their foot. This is a way of counting time, and enables them to maintain an even beat.

In this lesson we will learn how to use our foot to keep time. The accompanying diagram shows the proper technique of the foot beating the floor on the "Down Beat." At this point in our training, we will use a four count beat. We will count one, and two, and three, and four, and one, and two, and three, and four, and so on. On every count, our foot will tap the floor. Use any tempo you wish. In other words, tap your foot at any speed you desire; however, you must keep the beat even. Maintain a constant, even beat.

READING THE TIME SIGNATURE USING 3/4 TIME

In 3/4 time we use three beats to each measure. We can use three strokes or use one bass note and two strokes to play the rhythm.

COMMON OR 4/4 TIME

There are several time signatures in music; however, the one most frequently used is 4/4 time, also referred to as common time. Quite frequently composers will designate 4/4 time by using the capital C.

The diagram at the right shows one way of playing 4/4 rhythm. We can use four solid strokes, or we may alternate a bass note on the first and third beat.

SUGGESTION:

Check the tuning of your strings before you begin practicing. New strings will require frequent tuning.

THE STAFF — TIME SIGNATURE

THE STAFF

TREBLE CLEF

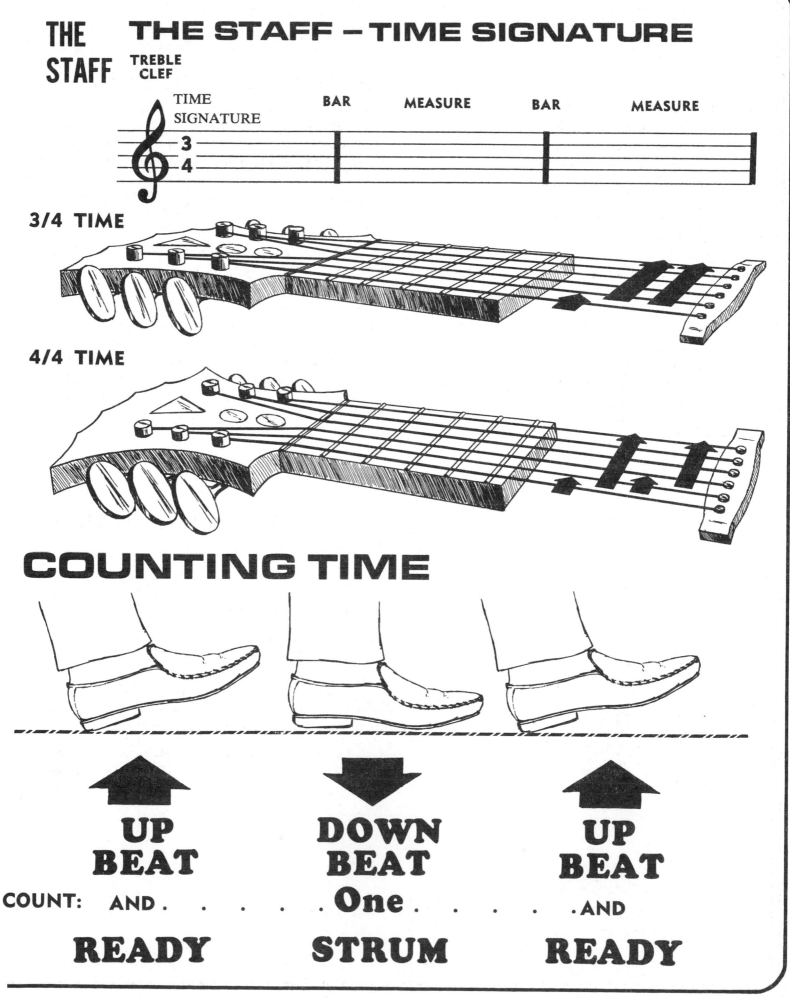

TIME SIGNATURE

BAR   MEASURE   BAR   MEASURE

3/4 TIME

4/4 TIME

COUNTING TIME

UP BEAT

DOWN BEAT

UP BEAT

COUNT: AND . . . . . . One . . . . . . AND

READY

STRUM

READY

CHORD THEORY

SCALES

BASIC CHORD THEORY

TEN DIGITS OF MATH

The new guitar student faces many difficult hours in learning how to successfully play the instrument. Quite often just getting past the sore finger stage is a fundamental task in itself. Since the student wants "to play", most all of his effort is spent in the art of getting recognizable sounds out of the instrument and little time is spent in understanding the music being played. Since many players become overwhelmed with all the technical aspects of music and can play without this knowledge, they let this important part of their music education go by them.

Music can be quite confusing. Not only do we have people applying their own names to music terminology, we also find that many specific musical terms have more than one theoretical name. Yet despite the apparent confusion there is a basic and simple philosophy to music. Music is in itself a science of mathematics and by using a mathematical approach we can better understand musical theory and as with math, learn to create with it.

All of our lives we have worked with mathematical problems ranging from simple arithmetic used in balancing our checkbook to the more complicated forms of math used by engineers and other professional people. Stop and consider how complicated math can be, yet the base of all math is TEN DIGITS—Zero through nine (Illustration 1). We have all learned to use these digits and do so daily.

In music we have only twelve notes (Illustration 2). These twelve notes have been used for hundreds of years and all of our great music is written with them. Classical, Jazz, or Country, we are using only these twelve notes. If we can learn to use the ten digits of math, certainly we can learn to use the twelve musical notes to improve our playing.

There are SEVEN letters in the musical alphabet—*A B C D E F G*. When we arrive at the note *G*, we start over again. These twelve notes are best represented by the piano keyboard. The white keys are the musical alphabet—*A B C D E F G*, repeating in sequence several times over. The black keys are the SHARPS and FLATS (Illustration 3).

ENHARMONIC CHANGE

"ENHARMONIC CHANGE"—One tone with two different "Spellings". Illustration three shows the complete twelve note musical alphabet, a "Chromatic Scale". Notice how the sharps and flats occur between all notes in the musical alphabet except the notes *BC* and *EF*. There are no sharps or flats between these tones. As written, the notes represent a complete Chromatic Scale, and it is possible to play them ascending or descending in pitch. In other words we can play up or down scale.

Between the notes *A* and *B* we have a half tone (Illustration 4). The half tone is written as *A#* or *B♭*. Since this tone sounds the same regardless of what we call it, why do we use two names? If we were playing the Chromatic Scale ascending in pitch we could call it *A#*. Descending in pitch it could be called *B♭*. By either name it is still found at the same fret on the guitar (Illustration 5).

ILLUSTRATION **1**

10 DIGITS OF MATH

0 1 2 3 4 5 6 7 8 9

ILLUSTRATION **2**

12 NOTES OF MUSIC

A	A#	B	C	C#	D	D#	E	F	F#	G	G#	A
1	2	3	4	5	6	7	8	9	10	11	12	OCTAVE

ILLUSTRATION **3**

ENHARMONIC CHANGES

UP SCALE   SHARP # ▶

A#		C#	D#		F#	G#	
A	B	C	D	E	F	G	A
B♭		D♭	E♭		G♭	A♭	

◀ DOWNSCALE   FLAT ♭

ILLUSTRATION **4**

ONE TONE WITH TWO NAMES

ILLUSTRATION **5**

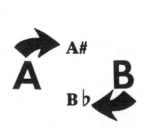

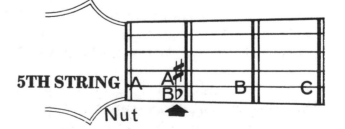

BASIC CHORD THEORY

THE CHROMATIC SCALE

The twelve notes of the musical alphabet played in succession, ascending or descending in pitch, is called a CHROMATIC SCALE. When the original tone is repeated, making thirteen notes, we have played one OCTAVE. Illustration one shows the complete Chromatic Scale, twelve tones plus the Octave note repeating the first note.

12 CHROMATIC SCALES

Since we have twelve notes in music we can have twelve Chromatic Scales, each starting on a different note in the scale. Illustration two shows these 12 scales. This is the basis of establishing our musical KEYS. If the first note of the scale is the note *A*, we would have the *"A Chromatic Scale"*.

THE CHROMATIC SCALE IN WRITTEN FORM

Illustration three shows how a Chromatic Scale appears in written form. While you may not be able to read music, try to compare the written form, Illustration three, with the alphabet, Illustration one. The *A Chromatic Scale* is written with Sharps as there are no flats in the *A Chromatic Scale*. (See page **26**, Key Signatures).

THE OCTAVE

When a string on the guitar is plucked we cause it to vibrate back and forth a certain number of times each second. The heavy strings, the 4th, 5th, and the 6th strings vibrate very slowly. The thin strings, the 3rd, 2nd, and the 1st strings vibrate much faster creating a higher pitch. The 5th string on the guitar is called the *A* string, and when tuned to proper pitch, vibrates 110 cycles per second. This is known as STANDARD PITCH for the guitar. Counting up twelve frets on the guitar we will have the *A* note again. However it will be one OCTAVE higher. Since the string has been shortened, we have increased the rate of vibration and the *A* note at the twelfth fret will be vibrating twice as fast or 220 cycles per second.

CHROMATIC SCALES

ILLUSTRATION **1**

THE CHROMATIC SCALE

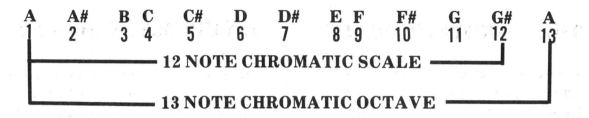

A	A#	B	C	C#	D	D#	E	F	F#	G	G#	A
1	2	3	4	5	6	7	8	9	10	11	12	13

12 NOTE CHROMATIC SCALE

13 NOTE CHROMATIC OCTAVE

ILLUSTRATION **2**

12 CHROMATIC SCALES

```
A A# B C C# D D# E F F# G G# A
A# B C C# D D# E F F# G G# A A#
B C C# D D# E F F# G G# A A# B
C C# D D# E F F# G G# A A# B C
C# D D# E F F# G G# A A# B C C#
D D# E F F# G G# A A# B C C# D
D# E F F# G G# A A# B C C# D D#
E F f # G G# A A# B C C# D D# E
F F# G G# A A# B C C# D D# E F
F# G G# A A# B C C# D D# E F F#
G G# A A# B C C# D D# E F F# G
G# A A# B C C# D D# E F F# G G#
```

ILLUSTRATION **3**

THE WRITTEN CHROMATIC SCALE

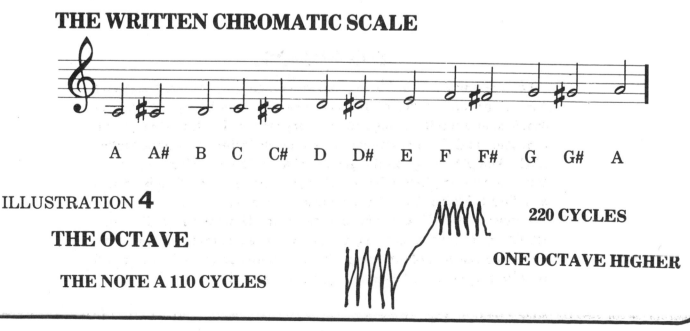

A   A#   B   C   C#   D   D#   E   F   F#   G   G#   A

ILLUSTRATION **4**

THE OCTAVE

THE NOTE A 110 CYCLES

220 CYCLES

ONE OCTAVE HIGHER

THE GUITAR FINGER BOARD SIX CHROMATIC SCALES

The piano has one Chromatic Scale repeating itself in higher and higher octaves with the lowest octave on the left side of the keyboard (Illustration at bottom of page). The white keys *A B C D E F G*, and the black keys, the sharps *A# C# D# F# G#*, or the flats *A♭ B♭ D♭ E♭ G♭*, make up the piano keyboard.

The guitar has six Chromatic Scales—six strings. The Chromatic Scale can start on any note in the scale, progressing till the thirteenth note repeats the first note again. On the guitar the Chromatic Scale starts with the open string and continues up the neck ascending in pitch till we repeat the first note (Open String) at the twelfth fret. Twelve frets plus the open string equals thirteen notes, one CHROMATIC OCTAVE.

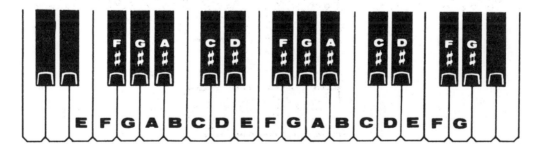

SIX CHROMATIC SCALES

THE COMPLETE GUITAR FINGER BOARD

(12 FRETS PLUS THE OPEN STRINGS)

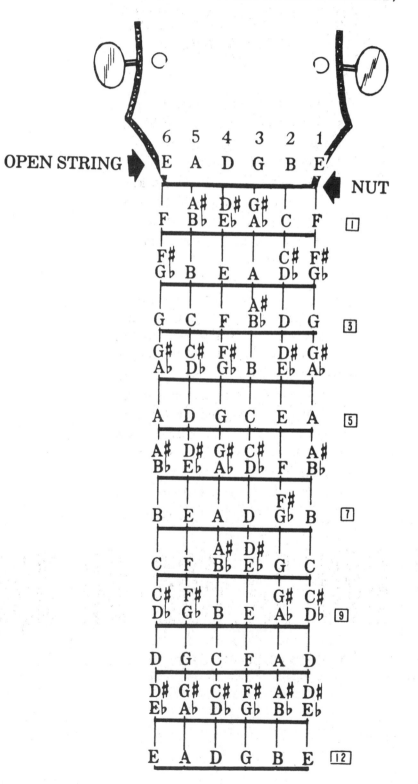

BASIC CHORD THEORY

WHAT IS A MAJOR DIATONIC SCALE?

The Chromatic Scale is the progression, in Half Steps, of all twelve musical notes with the thirteenth note repeating the first. However, most modern music is not written in the Chromatic Scale, but reduced to the more pleasant sounding DIATONIC SCALE.

The Major Diatonic Scale is a predetermined pattern of eight notes, arranged in five Whole Steps (Whole Tones) and two Half Steps (Semi Tones). A whole step is equal to two frets on the guitar, and a half step is the distance of one fret. In other words, a Major Diatonic Scale is a succession of tones arranged in a regular pattern. We hear this as a natural progression of tones when played on any musical instrument.

A Major Diatonic Scale can be built on any of the twelve notes of the Chromatic Scale. Thus we have twelve Major Scales called KEYS, each a different pitch. The Major Diatonic Scale covers the same tonal range as the Chromatic Scale of the same name, however it is made up of only eight of the thirteen notes. In order to eliminate the five unwanted notes from the Chromatic Scale, we use the STEP, STEP, HALF STEP principal (Illustration 1). Again, a Step is the distance of two frets on the guitar, a Half Step being the distance of one fret (Illustration 2).

NOTES ON THE FINGER BOARD—THE C SCALE

The student should experiment with the Step, Step, Half Step, Step, Step, Step, Half Step principal on the finger board. Start at any fret and walk up the finger board in this two Step, Half Step, three Step, Half Step progression as outlined in Illustration two. Your ending note should always be the same as your starting note. In playing the Major Diatonic Scale, use all four fingers—starting with the first finger on the first note, second finger on the second note, etc. When the fourth finger has played the Half Step, the fourth note, slide the hand down and use the first finger for the fifth note. In this manner the fourth finger will always play the Half Steps.

DEGREES OF THE SCALE

Music is a mathematical science and it is easier to comprehend Music Theory if we can develop a mathematical approach to notes, theory, chord construction, and chord progressions. As an example: Each step of the Diatonic Scale may be indicated by Roman numerals. This designation is used commonly in theory books relating to chord construction. Each Degree also has a proper theoretical name (Illustration 3). The terms TONIC, SUBDOMINANT, DOMINANT are also used to describe the three primary chords of each KEY. In 1812, Sara Ann Glover developed the SO-FA system to enable vocalists to sing Major Diatonic Scales, DO being the first note of the Scale (Illustration 3).

THE C DIATONIC SCALE IN WRITTEN FORM

Illustration four represents the C Major Diatonic Scale as it appears in written form. To familiarize the student with written music we have provided written material throughout this book.

Notice that the Diatonic Scale is comprised of TWO steps, Half Step, THREE steps, Half Step.

THE DIATONIC SCALE

THE MAJOR DIATONIC SCALE: 7 NOTES
THE MAJOR DIATONIC OCTAVE: 8 NOTES

ILLUSTRATION **1**

KEY OF C

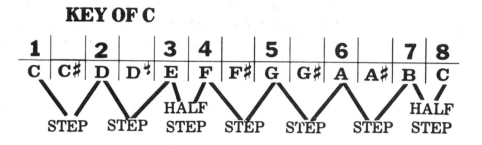

DIATONIC SCALE
CHROMATIC SCALE

ILLUSTRATION **2**

NOTES ON THE FINGER BOARD
C SCALE = STEP, STEP, HALF STEP

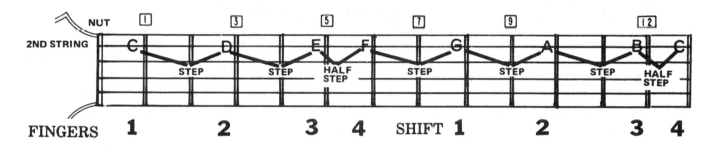

ILLUSTRATION **3**

DEGREES OF THE SCALE

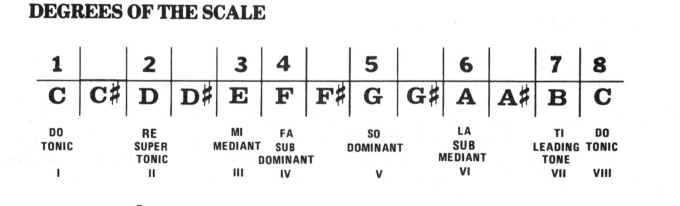

ILLUSTRATION **4**

C DIATONIC SCALE IN WRITTEN FORM

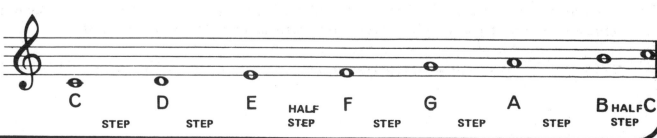

BASIC CHORD THEORY

THE C MAJOR DIATONIC SCALE

There are seven different terms used in reference to each note of the eight note Major DIATONIC Scale (Illustration 1).

ALPHABETICAL

Each Diatonic Scale will have a different group of letters and a different arrangement and number of sharps or flats. In the example shown, the C Scale—C D EF G A BC, there are no sharps or flats as the C Scale is the Natural Scale.

SCALE DEGREES

Each note of the scale is called a DEGREE, and may be indicated by ARABIC Numerals— 1 2 3 4 5 6 7 8.

Each degree may also be indicated by ROMAN Numerals—I II III IV V VI VII VIII. The usage of Roman numerals is common in theory studies.

THE DO RE MI SYSTEM

Developed by Sara Ann Glover in 1812, this system is utilized by voice teachers to train students in singing Major Diatonic Scales.

THEORETICAL FORM

The correct theoretical name for each degree of the scale (Tonic, Super Tonic, Mediant, Subdominant, Dominant, Submediant, Leading Tone, Tonic) are commonly used in chord theory studies.

INTERVALS

An INTERVAL is the distance between two tones. There are Major, Minor, Diminished, Augmented, and Perfect intervals. Abbreviations such as P.P. for Perfect Prime, Ma2 for Major second, P.4 for Perfect fourth are quite often used in substitution for written interval names.

THE DIATONIC SCALE EXTENDED TWO OCTAVES

The Major Diatonic Scale, eight notes, can be continued on in higher or lower sequence called OCTAVES. It is permissible to continue counting numerically— 9 10 11 12 13 14 15—to determine the next Octave (Illustration 2). The first and eighth notes are the same alphabetically, as are the second and ninth, third and tenth, etc. (Illustration 3).

When building "Extended" chords, 9th, 11th, 13th, this continuation of the Major Diatonic Scale is utilized to determine these additional notes.

WRITTEN FORM

In Illustration four, we show how this two octave extended Major Diatonic Scale appears in musical notation.

THE DIATONIC SCALE
THEORETICAL FORM

ILLUSTRATION **1**

THE C MAJOR DIATONIC SCALE

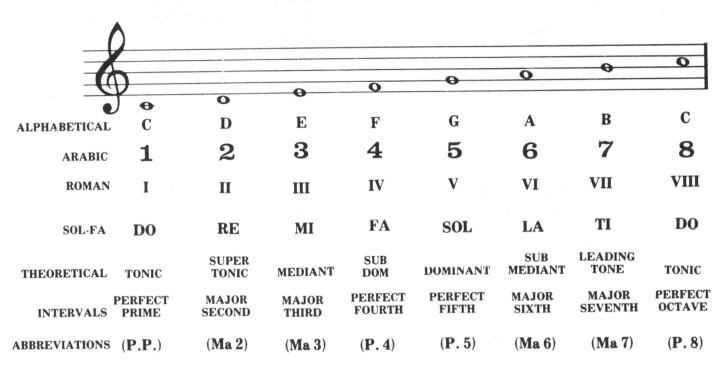

ALPHABETICAL	C	D	E	F	G	A	B	C
ARABIC	1	2	3	4	5	6	7	8
ROMAN	I	II	III	IV	V	VI	VII	VIII
SOL-FA	DO	RE	MI	FA	SOL	LA	TI	DO
THEORETICAL	TONIC	SUPER TONIC	MEDIANT	SUB DOM	DOMINANT	SUB MEDIANT	LEADING TONE	TONIC
INTERVALS	PERFECT PRIME	MAJOR SECOND	MAJOR THIRD	PERFECT FOURTH	PERFECT FIFTH	MAJOR SIXTH	MAJOR SEVENTH	PERFECT OCTAVE
ABBREVIATIONS	(P.P.)	(Ma 2)	(Ma 3)	(P. 4)	(P. 5)	(Ma 6)	(Ma 7)	(P. 8)

ILLUSTRATION **2**

THE DIATONIC SCALE EXTENDED TWO OCTAVES

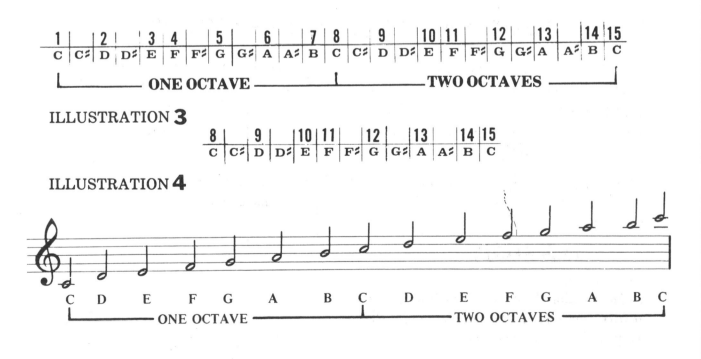

ILLUSTRATION **3**

ILLUSTRATION **4**

WRITING MAJOR DIATONIC SCALES

As an aid to understanding chord theory the student should be able to quickly write the Major Diatonic Scale for any Key. To write the Diatonic Scale, first draw a horizontal line, then place twelve short vertical lines, spaced evenly, on the horizontal line (Illustration 1).

Next, write in the eight numbers as shown on the top of the horizontal line allowing for the proper spacing for the Steps and Half Steps. Observe the space between each number with the exception of the third and fourth, and the seventh and eighth degrees. This corresponds to the Step, Half Step principal (Illustration 2). Next, write in the Chromatic Scale, starting with the Key note desired. In this example we start with the note *A*. The *A Major Diatonic Scale* will be those notes directly under the eight degrees of the scale.

Illustrations four, five, and six show three more Keys. By writing these scales the student can quickly see the placement of the sharps or flats within each Key. For example, the Key of D Major has two sharps—*F#* number three, and *C#* number seven (Illustration 4).

KEY SIGNATURES

The Key of *E Major* has four sharps (Illustration 5). The Key of *G Major* has one sharp (Illustration 6). Observe that the Chromatic Scale has not changed in any way. Only the starting note is different for each Key.

Being able to write out the Diatonic Scales will enable the student to establish all Key Signatures.

BUILDING THE DIATONIC SCALE

WRITING MAJOR DIATONIC SCALES

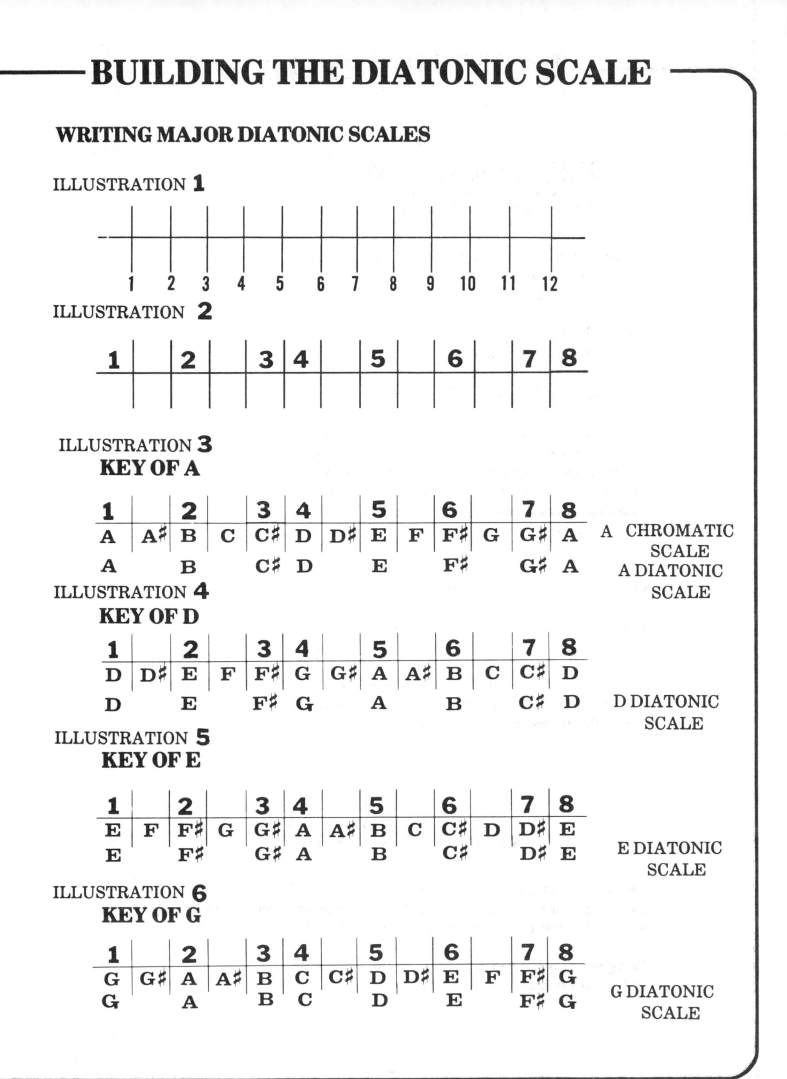

HOW TO READ
WRITTEN CHORDS

The importance of note reading can not be over emphasized. If you are seeking information about music, you must have some knowledge of note reading. It is not necessary to be able to read and play instantly, in other words "sight read", but any serious student of the guitar should become familiar with the basic principals of note reading to better understand written explanations.

Written notes may be read two ways—VERTICAL-LY and HORIZONTALLY. A series of single notes written HORIZONTALLY is referred to as a MELODY (Illustration 1). Chords are a combination of three or more tones played together at one time. Consequently, notes written VERTICALLY are called CHORDS (Illustration 2).

When playing a melody we pick a series of notes one after another. When notes are stacked vertically we must play them all together at one time. This is accomplished by "strumming".

MELODIES READ HORIZONTALLY

Illustration three shows three melody notes—*E G C* written horizontally. They would be played one at a time reading from left to right.

CHORDS READ VERTICALLY

Illustration four shows these same notes—*E G C*, written vertically which would be played together as a Chord.

READING WRITTEN CHORDS

ILLUSTRATION **1**

MELODY: READING HORIZONTALLY

ILLUSTRATION **2**

CHORDS: READING VERTICALLY

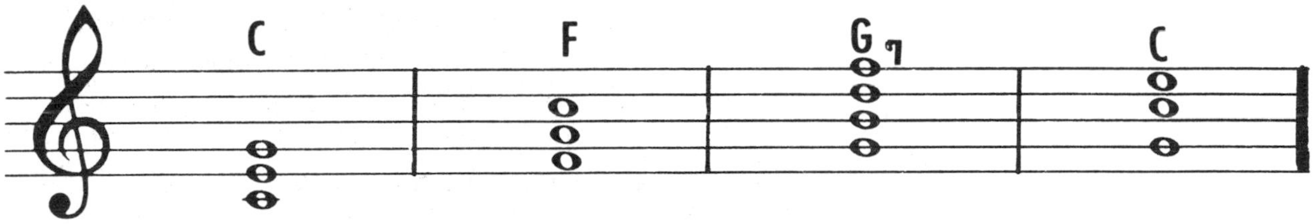

ILLUSTRATION **3**

MELODY:

A SUCCESSION OF SINGLE TONES

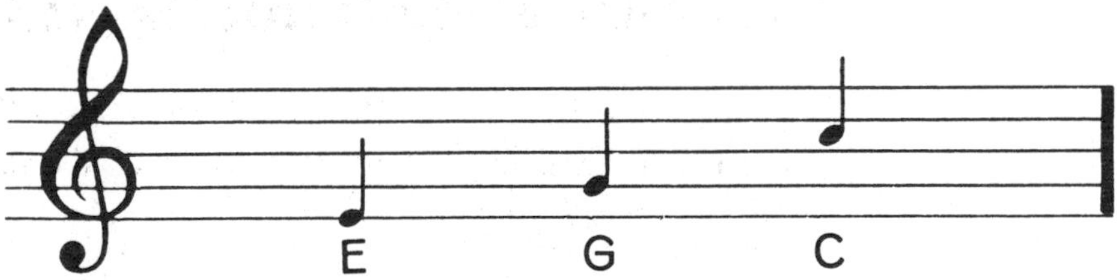

ILLUSTRATION **4**

CHORDS:

A COMBINATION OF TONES SOUNDED TOGETHER

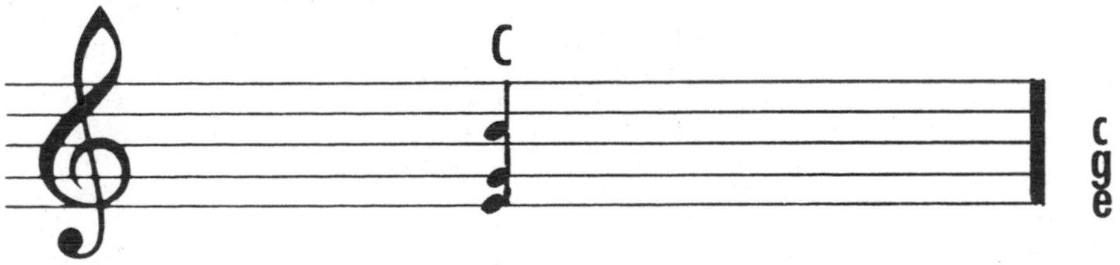

C CHORD TRIAD

BASIC CHORD THEORY

WHAT ARE CHORDS

A chord is the simultaneous sounding of THREE or more tones. There are many types of chords and many variations or each. We have MAJOR, MINOR, DIMINISHED, AUGMENTED, and DOMINANT chords, plus variations such as 6ths, 7ths, 9ths, 11ths, and 13ths.

TRIADS

By superimposing the First, Third and Fifth notes of the *C Scale*, we have constructed the *C* chord with the notes *c e g*. These three notes are called a TRIAD. Triads may be written different ways (Illustration 1). For example: One, Three and Five—Root, 3rd, and 5th—and Root, Major 3rd, Perfect 5th (See INTERVALS).

THE MAJOR CHORD

The MAJOR CHORD Triad consists of three tones, and is formed by combining the fundamental tone, the first note of a Major Diatonic Scale, with the Third and Fifth notes of the Scale. The first tone of the scale, the TONIC note, is known as the ROOT of the chord. Thus the formula for building all Major chord triads can be stated simply as combining the Root, 3rd and 5th (Illustration 2).

TRIAD AS WRITTEN ON STAFF

Illustration three shows how these three notes appear on the staff in written form. Illustration four shows the three notes written as a chord triad. Notice that the lowest sounding note of a chord will appear as the bottom note when written on the staff. When holding the guitar, the lowest note of the chord will be on one of the lower strings and is the first note sounded when strumming. Illustration Five shows finger placement to play this chord.

MAJOR CHORD TRIAD

ILLUSTRATION 1

MAJOR CHORDS ARE BUILT UPON THE:

			NOTES OF THE
1ST	3RD	AND 5TH	MAJOR DIATONIC SCALE

ALSO CALLED   ROOT   3RD   &   5TH

ILLUSTRATION 2

C CHORD TRIAD   1 3 5 [C E G]

1		2		3	4		5		6		7	8
C	C♯	D	D♯	E	F	F♯	G	G♯	A	A♯	B	C

ROOT C   E   G = C CHORD TRIAD

ILLUSTRATION 3

TRIAD FROM WRITTEN SCALE

C   D   E   F   G   A   B   C

1   3   5

ILLUSTRATION 4

TRIAD AS WRITTEN ON STAFF

ILLUSTRATION 5

C CHORD

R C E G C E

THE MAJOR CHORD

The Major chord is built on the first, third, and fifth notes of the Major Diatonic Scale. In Illustration one, the *A* Scale, the three notes that form the *A* Major Chord are—*A C# E*.

These notes may be repeated and may be in any order, but only these three notes make the *A* Major chord. (See **INVERSIONS** Page 46).

MINOR CHORDS

The Minor chord is built on the first, lowered third (flatted third), and the fifth of the Major Diatonic Scale. In Illustration two the *A* Minor chord is built on the notes *A C E*.

ILLUSTRATION 1

A MAJOR CHORD

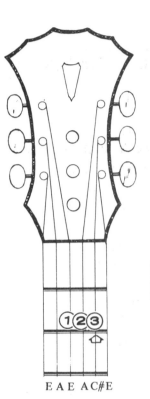

E A E AC#E

R 3 5
A C# E

A DIATONIC SCALE

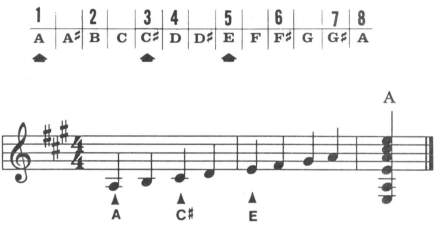

1		2		3	4		5	6		7	8
A	A#	B	C	C#	D	D#	E	F	F#	G	G#	A

ILLUSTRATION 2

A MINOR CHORD

R♭3 5
A C E

A DIATONIC SCALE

1		2		3	4		5	6		7	8
A	A#	B	C	C#	D	D#	E	F	F#	G	G#	A

E A E AC E

DOMINANT 7TH CHORDS

The Dominant 7th chord is a four tone chord built by forming a Major chord triad (R 3 5) and then adding a lowered seventh note of the scale to the Triad. A note is flatted by lowering its pitch one half tone. To demonstrate this, form the Chord *C* (Illustration 1). Our basic Triad, R 3 5, will be the notes *c e g*. To construct a *C*7th chord, we count up to the seventh degree of the scale which is the note *B*. Lowering this one fret, a Half Step, we have *B♭*. The note *B♭* can be added to the *C* chord by using the little finger. Observe that by playing the *B♭* on the third string we have eliminated the note *G*, our fifth note of the triad. This is permissable in chord construction. Should you prefer to add the note *G* back to the chord, you may fret the sixth string at the third fret with the third finger as shown in Illustration two.

Illustrations three and four show how we determine the notes that form the *G* Major Chord, and how the fingering must be changed to add the flatted seventh to change this chord from *G* to *G*7.

DOMINANT SEVENTH CHORDS

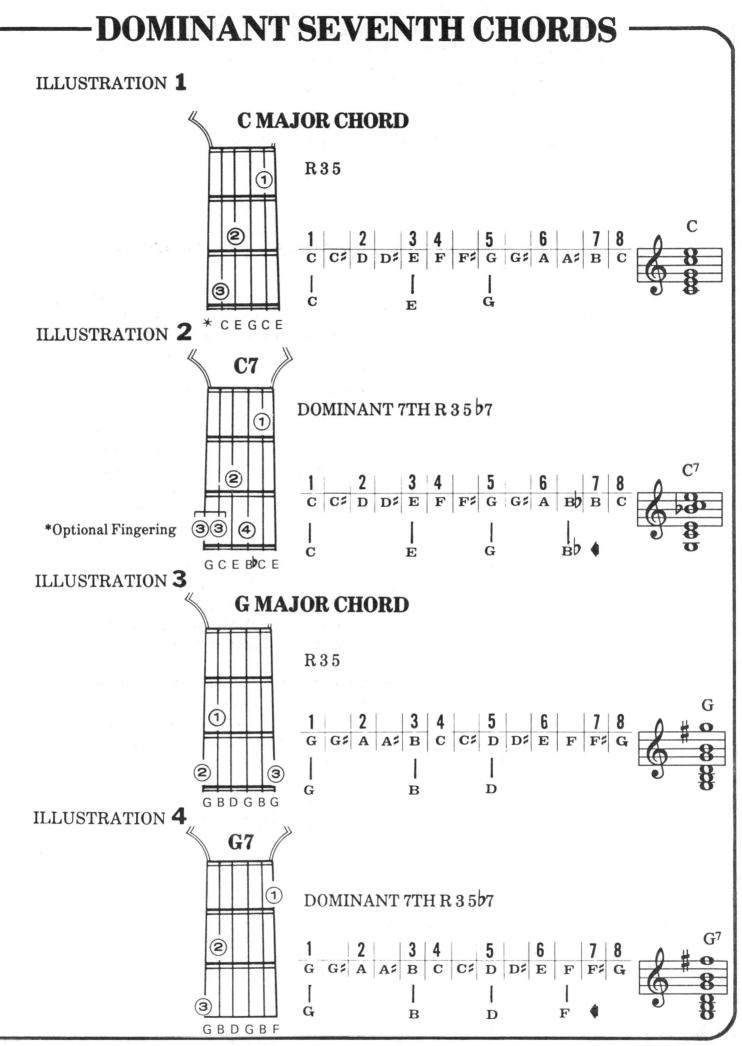

ILLUSTRATION **1**

C MAJOR CHORD

R 3 5

1		2		3	4		5		6		7	8
C	C♯	D	D♯	E	F	F♯	G	G♯	A	A♯	B	C
C				E			G					

C

* C E G C E

ILLUSTRATION **2**

C7

DOMINANT 7TH R 3 5 ♭7

*Optional Fingering

1		2		3	4		5		6		7	8
C	C♯	D	D♯	E	F	F♯	G	G♯	A	B♭	B	C
C				E			G			B♭		

C⁷

G C E B♭ C E

ILLUSTRATION **3**

G MAJOR CHORD

R 3 5

1		2		3	4		5		6		7	8
G	G♯	A	A♯	B	C	C♯	D	D♯	E	F	F♯	G
G				B			D					

G

G B D G B G

ILLUSTRATION **4**

G7

DOMINANT 7TH R 3 5 ♭7

1		2		3	4		5		6		7	8
G	G♯	A	A♯	B	C	C♯	D	D♯	E	F	F♯	G
G				B			D			F		

G⁷

G B D G B F

THE DOMINANT 9TH CHORDS

The Dominant 9th chord is a Dominant type chord. The formula for building a Dominant 9th chord is: R 3 5 ♭7 plus the added ninth note of the Major Diatonic scale. How do we find a ninth note? We simply start counting over again as shown in Illustration one. Since the first and eighth degrees have the same name, actually they are the same note one octave apart in the scale, we merely go back to the Tonic degree and continue counting upward. (See Page **22**).

THE DOMINANT 13TH CHORD

The Dominant 13th chord is a popular Jazz chord and is used by Jazz, Blues and Orchestra guitarists. Like the 9th chord the 13th chord is a Dominant type chord—R 3 5 ♭7 plus the the 9th and 13th notes of the Major Diatonic scale added.

THE MAJOR 7TH CHORD

The student should be aware that there are two types of 7th chords. The Dominant 7th and the Major 7th. The Dominant 7th triad is R 3 5 ♭7. The Major 7th chord is built on the R 3 5 7. There is only one half tone's difference between the two chords.

The Major 7th chord is used extensively in modern music as a substitution for the Tonic chord, a Major chord.

DOMINANT 9TH AND 13TH CHORDS

ILLUSTRATION **1**

THE DOMINANT 9TH CHORD

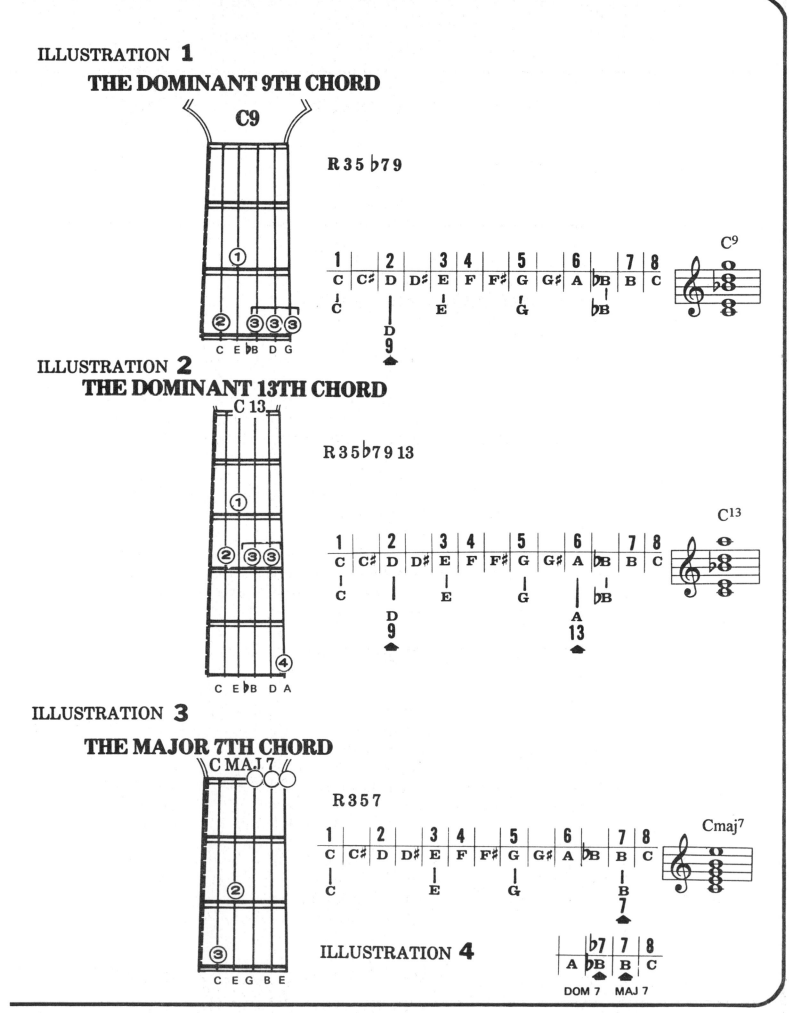

BUILDING THE AUGMENTED CHORD

The Augmented chord is a very unusual chord. Used properly it can be a substitute for the Dominant seventh chord. The Augmented chord may be written as AUG, or simply written as +5.

The formula for the Augmented chord is—R 3 +5 (Raised fifth). The term Augmented is used to denote the raising in pitch of a given note one half step, or one fret on the guitar (Illustration 3). Augmented chords are four string chords and can be moved up or down the neck becoming a different Augmented chord at every fret. Every FOURTH fret the chord will repeat itself, in other words the same notes will repeat although they will be arranged in different order.

In the Key of *A* the Augmented formula, R 3 +5 (Illustration 1), will produce the notes *A C# E#*. NOTE: The Enharmonic name for *E#* is *F*. In Illustration two, the chord *A* Major, R 3 5, is built with the notes *A C# E*. By raising the 5th of the Triad, we have the *A* Augmented chord (Illustration 3). The student should associate this altered Major chord Triad with the Augmented chord. If you know how to play the *A* Major chord, you will know the *A* Augmented chord as well.

THE AUGMENTED CHORD
AUGMENTED CHORD FORMULA
R 3#5

ILLUSTRATION **1**   **KEY OF A**

THE A AUGMENTED CHORD R 3 #5 A C#E#

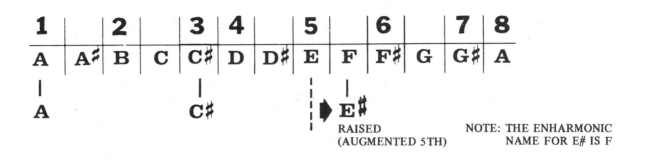

1	2		3	4		5		6		7	8
A	A#	B	C	C#	D	D#	E	F	F#	G	G#	A

A — A

C# — C#

E# RAISED (AUGMENTED 5TH)

NOTE: THE ENHARMONIC NAME FOR E# IS F

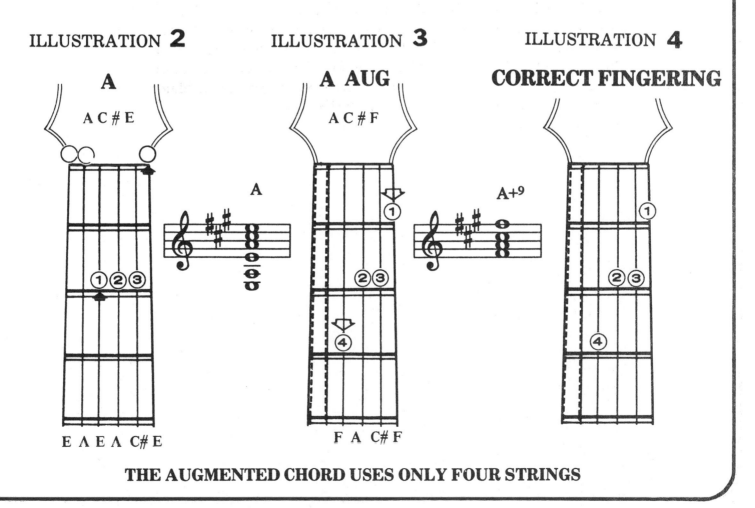

ILLUSTRATION **2**   ILLUSTRATION **3**   ILLUSTRATION **4**

A   **A AUG**   **CORRECT FINGERING**

A C # E   A C # F

E Λ E Λ C# E   F A C# F

THE AUGMENTED CHORD USES ONLY FOUR STRINGS

THE AUGMENTED CHORD—
ONE CHORD-THREE TRIADS

The AUGMENTED chord is a series of Major 3rd intervals played one above another and consists of the Root, Major 3rd, and an Augmented or raised 5th (See INTERVALS, advanced chord theory). It is very flexible in that it has no strong root because of the altered 5th. The Augmented chord can be easily recognized as it is the only chord with two Major 3rds above each other. FORMULA for the AUGMENTED CHORD (R 3 5#).

Another reason for the Augmented chord's flexibility is that each Augmented chord has three names. Any note in the chord's triad can be the name of the chord.

Illustration one shows the *F* Augmented chord built upon the R 3 5# notes of the *F* Diatonic Scale—*F A C#.*

In the Key of *A* the Augmented triad is *A C# F.* The same notes, by formula, in each of these three Keys makes the same chord. Consequently, one chord has a strong resolution to all three Keys.

The name of the Augmented chord is determined by the location of the Root note. By learning one Augmented chord, you have really learned three chords, since the Root can be any note of the chord.

The augmented chord repeats itself every FOUR frets—the same notes reappear.

AUGMENTED TRIADS

THE AUGMENTED CHORD: R 3#5
EACH POSITION CONSISTS OF THREE TRIADS

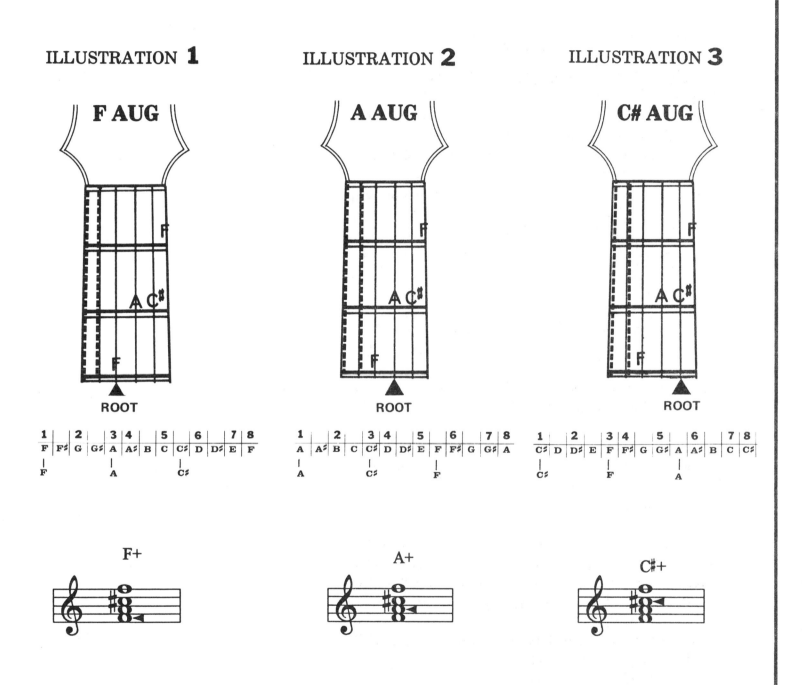

ILLUSTRATION **1**　　ILLUSTRATION **2**　　ILLUSTRATION **3**

F AUG　　　　A AUG　　　　C# AUG

F+　　　　A+　　　　C#+

Each triad consists of the same notes, within their respective scales. Only their sequence is different when played. We merely place the "Root" on a different string to name each chord.

DIMINISHED CHORDS

The Diminished seventh chord is noted for its unusual sound and in modern music is used frequently. In the more basic chord progressions such as often used in Folk and Country music, the Diminished chord is seldom found.

The Diminished seventh chord is an altered Dominant 7th chord. It is constructed by lowering one half step the 3rd, 5th and the 7th notes of a Dominant 7th chord. The formula for constructing Diminished chords (Illustration 1) is: Root $\flat$3 , $\flat$5 , 6th ($\flat\flat$7). The student should keep in mind that a Dominant 7th chord is constructed with a flatted 7th. When building the Diminished chord we lower this note again to the 6th note of the scale, actually making it a DOUBLE FLAT.

The Diminished 7th chord can be abbreviated as follows: DIM, DIM7, or simply as: 0, or 07. Example—the *C* DIM chord could be written as: *Co7, C DIM, C DIM7.*

The Diminished triad is easily recognized as it is the only triad with two Minor 3rds above each other.

Illustration two shows the more common fingering used to play the Diminished chord. This is a four string chord with the Root note in the bass (lowest string of the chord). Illustration three shows proper fingering to play the chord. In this form the chord is a movable chord and can be moved up and down the neck. The name of the chord is determined by the name of the note that the Root of the chord is on, as any one of the four notes may be considered the Root tone.

THE DIMINISHED CHORD

THE DIMINISHED CHORD FORMULA

R ♭3 ♭5 6 [♭♭7]

KEY OF E   E DIMINISHED CHORD 1 ♭3 ♭5 6   E G ♭B C♯

ILLUSTRATION **1**

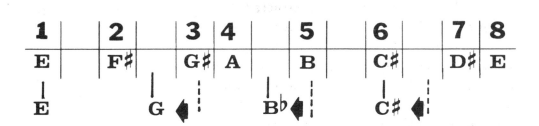

1	2	3	4	5	6	7	8
E	F♯	G♯	A	B	C♯	D♯	E
E		G		B♭	C♯		

ILLUSTRATION **2**   ILLUSTRATION **3**
                              CORRECT
E DIM   **FINGER POSITION**

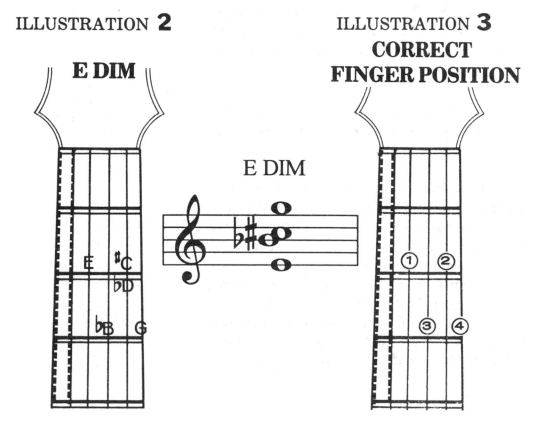

E DIM

THE DIMINISHED CHORD—
ONE CHORD-FOUR CHORD TRIADS

The Diminished chord is a four note chord. Each Diminished chord position will have four possible names as any note in the Diminished chord can be the Root note. In Illustration one, we show the E Diminished chord. It is an E Diminished chord because our Root note is E. Observe the E Diatonic Scale below the illustration. The E Diminished chord is: $E\ G\ A\#\ C\#$ In Illustration two we have made it into a $B\flat$ Diminished chord simply by moving the Root over to the third string and this is the $B\flat$ note. Observe the $B\flat$ Diatonic scale, the same Diminished chord formula applied to the $B\flat$ scale produces the same notes as in the above E scale. Only their sequence differs.

In Illustration three we have moved the Root to the 2nd string, and again we have the same four notes produced from the $D\flat$ scale. By moving the Root to the first string (Illustration 4) we have a G Diminished chord. Since each chord position can have four names, the chord is strongly related to each of the four Keys represented by these four notes. By simply learning one chord position, you know how to play four different Diminished chords. The Diminished chord repeats itself every THREE frets—the same notes reappear.

ENHARMONIC CHANGE

While each scale will produce the same notes, their spelling will differ. $D\flat$, $C\#$—$B\flat$, $A\#$; still the same notes.

44

DIMINISHED CHORD

THE DIMINISHED CHORD

EACH POSITION CONSISTS OF FOUR CHORDS

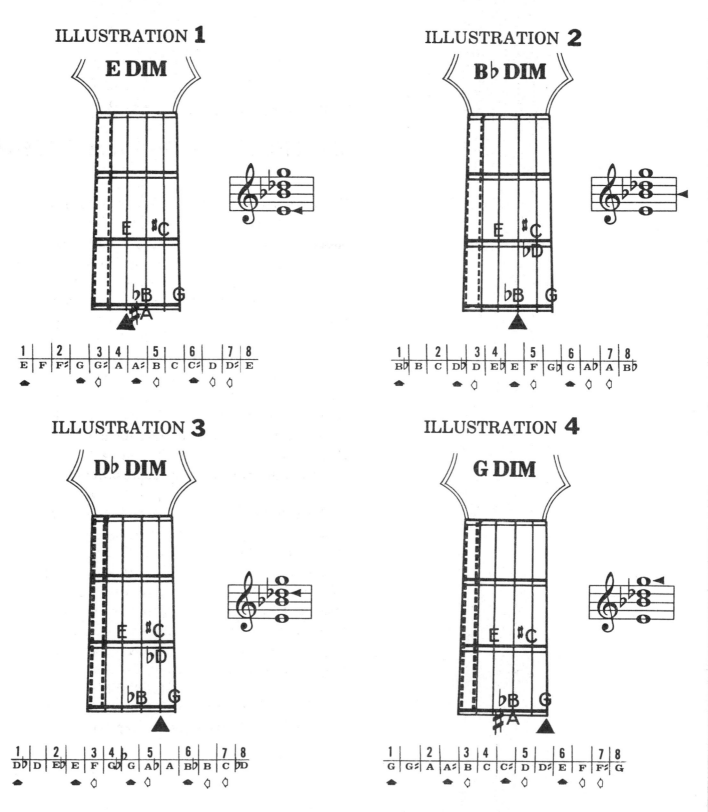

Each chord consists of the same notes within their respective scales. Only their sequence is different when played. The "Root" is on a different string for each chord.

BASIC CHORD THEORY

CHORD INVERSION

Notes that form the Triad of a chord are normally written: R 3 5. That is to say the Root note is written first with the third note next and the fifth note following it. Actually each Triad may be written three ways: R 3 5, 3 5 R, and 5 R 3. When any note of the triad other than the Root note appears as the lower voice, we have an INVERSION.

ROOT POSITION

When the Root of the chord (Illustration 1) is the lowest note, the chord is said to be in the Root Position.

FIRST INVERSION

When the third note of the chord is the lowest note of the triad, it is called the First Inversion (Illustration 2).

SECOND INVERSION

When the fifth note of the chord appears as the lowest note of the triad, the chord is in the Second Inversion (Illustration 3).

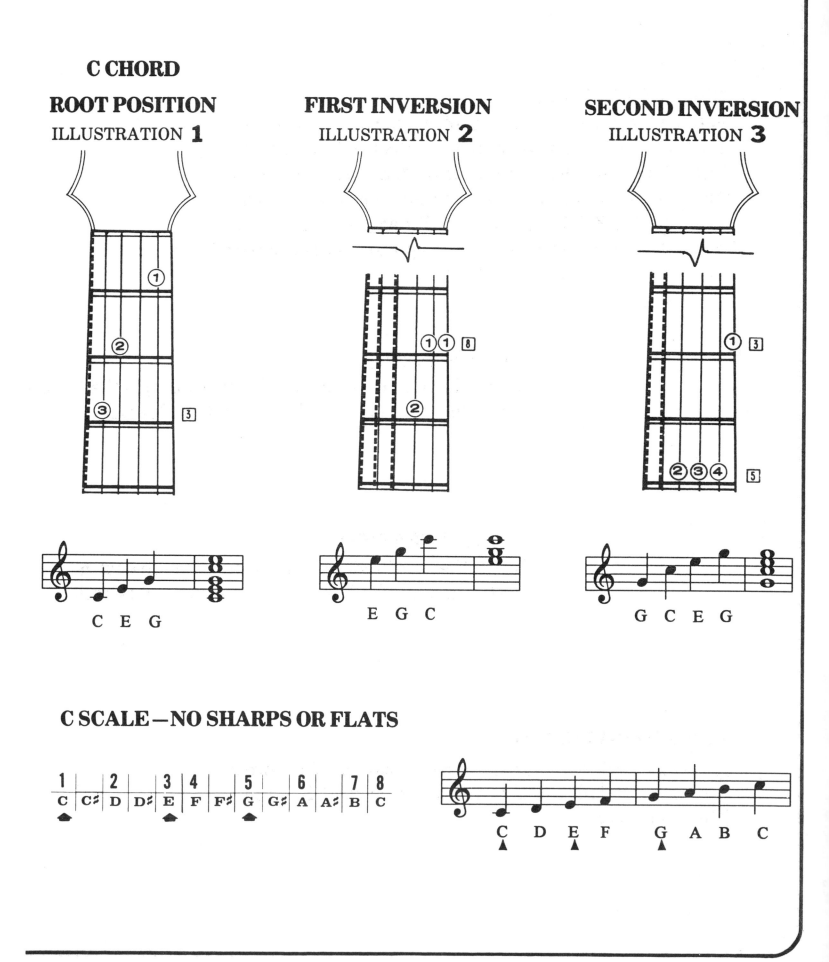

C CHORD

ROOT POSITION
ILLUSTRATION **1**

FIRST INVERSION
ILLUSTRATION **2**

SECOND INVERSION
ILLUSTRATION **3**

C E G

E G C

G C E G

C SCALE—NO SHARPS OR FLATS

1	2	3	4	5	6	7	8
C C♯	D D♯	E F	F♯	G G♯	A A♯	B	C

C D E F G A B C

BASIC CHORD THEORY

HARMONIZING WITH PRIMARY CHORDS

The term MELODY denotes an organized succession of three or more tones. Vocallists can sing only one note at a time, and by singing a succession of notes can sing what is commonly called the MELODY, or the LEAD. Illustration one represents a melody rising and falling in pitch as it might look on an electronic oscilloscope.

A CHORD is a series of three or more tones played together at one time. Since the guitar has six strings it is possible to play six notes together in what we refer to as a CHORD. While we may play all six strings at one time when strumming, we are in fact only playing three notes, as several of the notes will be duplicated in higher or lower octaves.

Illustration two represents a chord, six tones, as seen on an oscilloscope. Since a melody will be a succession of tones rising and falling in pitch with a large degree of variation between the higher and lower tones, it is not possible to use only one chord for playing rhythm. A chord must harmonize with the melody notes. This is to say that each melody note must be one of the notes of the chord Triad, or closely related to it. When the melody no longer harmonizes with the chord, we must change chords (Illustration 3).

THREE PRIMARY CHORDS

Most of our contemporary music of today can be harmonized with three chords (Illustration 4), chords built on the first, fourth, and fifth notes of the Diatonic scale. These three chords are written as the I IV V chords of each Key. The triads of the three primary chords of each Key contain all of the notes of that Major Diatonic Scale.

FORMULA FOR FINDING THE
THREE PRIMARY CHORDS

The name of the three primary chords to each Key can be determined by applying the formula—I IV V to the Major Diatonic Scale (Illustration 5).

To better understand chords construction, write a Diatonic Scale (Illustration 5). We have used the *C* Scale. The Tonic chord will always be the first chord or the I chord, and is built on the first note of the Scale. The SUBDOMINANT chord will be the IV chord and is built on the fourth note of the scale. The fifth note of the scale is the V chord and is called the DOMINANT CHORD. As you can see these three chords contain all eight notes of the *C* Major Diatonic Scale.

PRIMARY CHORDS TO EACH KEY

ILLUSTRATION **1**

MELODY: ONE NOTE

ILLUSTRATION **2**

CHORD: SIX TONES

(GUITAR)

ILLUSTRATION **3**

MELODY AND CHORDS

CHORD

MELODY

TONIC

4

SUB DOM

5

DOM

TONIC

ILLUSTRATION **4**

3 PRIMARY CHORDS TO EACH KEY

I	4	5	I
TONIC	SUB DOM	DOM	TONIC
C	F	G	C

ILLUSTRATION **5**

FORMULA FOR FINDING 3 PRIMARY CHORDS

FORMULA 1 4 5

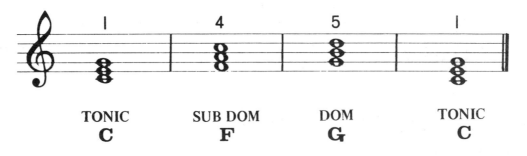

TONIC				SUB DOM		DOM					
1	**2**	**3**	**4**		**5**		**6**		**7**	**8**	
C	C♯	D	D♯	E	F	F♯	G	G♯	A	A♯	B	C
I			F		G						
C			F		G						

THE DOMINANT CHORD
LOWERED ONE OCTAVE

If you play the three primary chords to any Key, you will find the Dominant chord will normally sound lower than the Tonic (Key) chord. The Dominant chord is built on the fifth note of the scale and should sound higher than the Tonic chord which is built on the first note of the Scale. However in most basic chord progressions we normally lower the Dominant chord one octave (Illustration 1).

Illustration two shows the lowered octave arrangement of the Dominant chord triad. This is accomplished by placing the Root tone of the Dominant chord below the Tonic Chord.

—THE DOMINANT LOWERED ONE OCTAVE—

**DOMINANT CHORD
LOWERED ONE OCTAVE**

**V
DOM**

**IV
SUB DOM**

ILLUSTRATION **1**

**I
TONIC**

TONIC

**DOM
LOWERED
ONE OCTAVE**

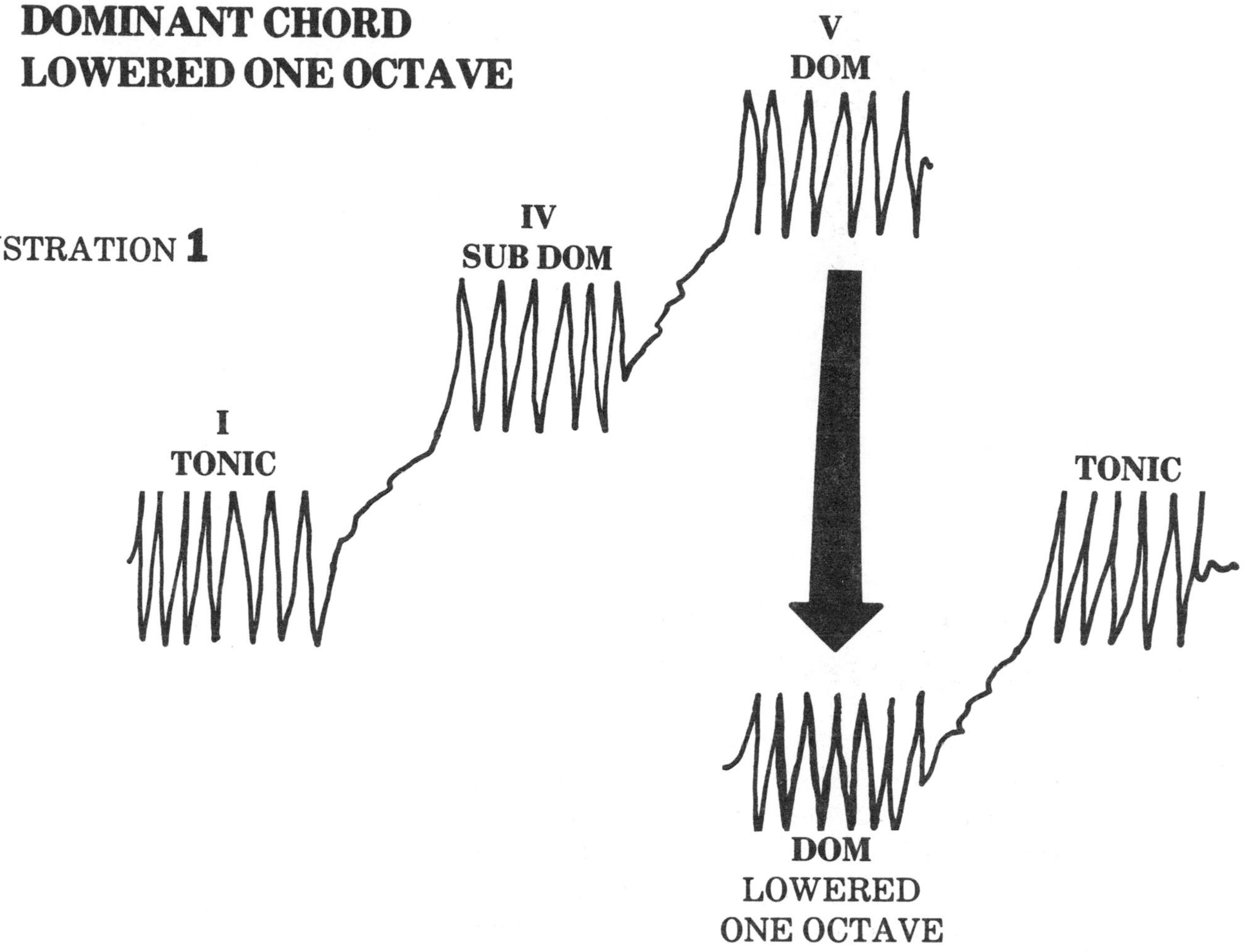

ILLUSTRATION **2**

C	F	G	G	C
I	IV	V	V	1
TONIC	SUB DOM	DOM	DOM LOWERED	TONIC

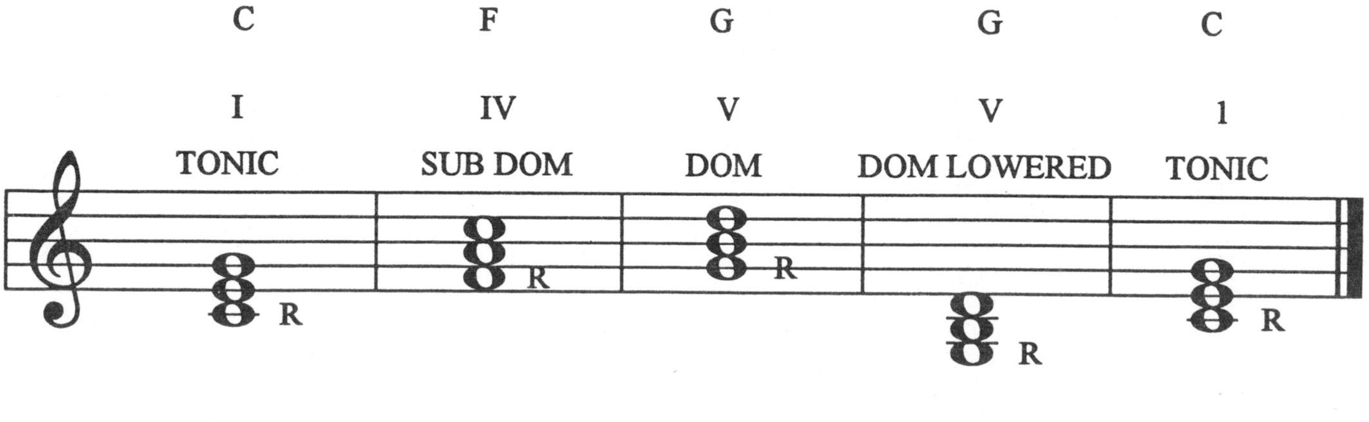

SCALE OF TRIADS

How do we know what chords belong to each Key? Composers and arrangers have simple rules to aid them in writing harmony, and to know and understand these rules will make all guitarists better musicians. To establish the chords that harmonize with notes of each Key we use the SCALE OF TRIADS. A Triad is a series of three tones played simultaneously to form a chord.

To establish the scale of triads, we first write a Diatonic Scale (Illustration 2). We then construct a three tone chord on each note of the scale. To build the chords we take a note of the scale and add every other note of the scale to it.

Another way to build the scale of triads is to write out three parallel scales. If we take the Key of C (Illustration 3), and write three parallel scales starting on C, E, and G, we then have three parallel scales called the SCALE OF TRIADS.

The seven harmonizing chords constructed in this manner are the basis upon which all harmony is built.

SCALE OF TRIADS

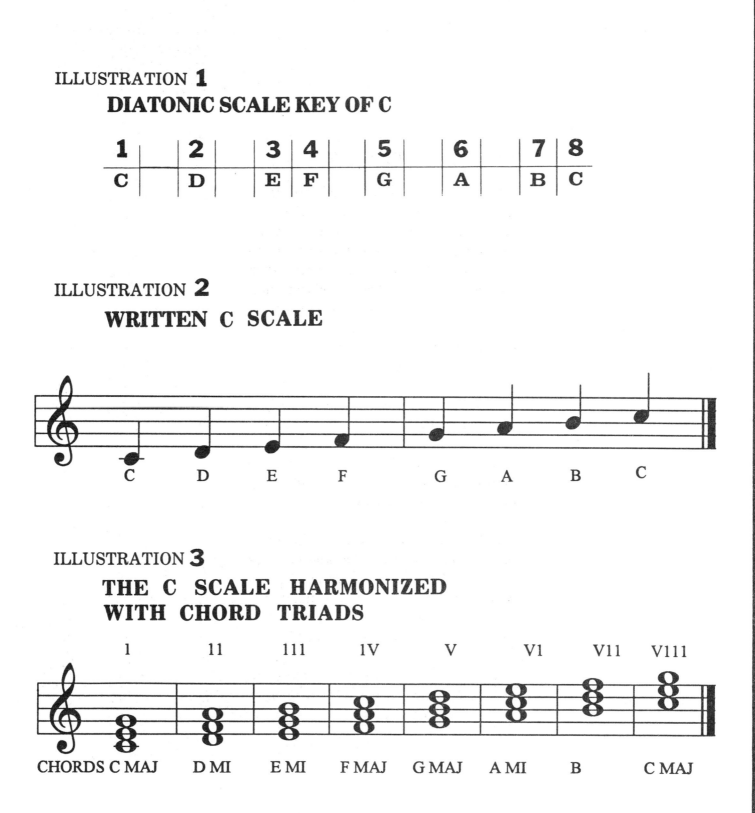

ILLUSTRATION **1**
DIATONIC SCALE KEY OF C

1	2	3	4	5	6	7	8
C	D	E	F	G	A	B	C

ILLUSTRATION **2**
WRITTEN C SCALE

C D E F G A B C

ILLUSTRATION **3**
THE C SCALE HARMONIZED
WITH CHORD TRIADS

1	11	111	1V	V	V1	V11	V111

CHORDS C MAJ   D MI   E MI   F MAJ   G MAJ   A MI   B   C MAJ

The scale harmonized with triads as shown is, in a large way, the basis upon which all harmony is built.

RELATED MINOR CHORDS

If rhythm guitarists were limited only to Major chords the chord progressions would be restricted and lack interesting tone coloration.

While the rhythm pattern to many songs is built around the three primary chords to each Key, we do have seven basic chords available in each Key as seen in the scale of triads on the preceeding page. The three primary chords are the Tonic—number one, the Subdominant—number four, and the Dominant—the number five chord.

The II chord, the III chord and VI chords are Minor chords and are called RELATED MINOR chords (Illustration 1). These three Minor chords are related because each is constructed on a note of the Major scale. In this example, the C Scale, each chord triad will be constructed with only notes of this scale. As an example, the A Minor chord is built with the notes A C E notes of the C Scale.

When you hear a Minor chord used in a song, look first for the VI chord, as it is the more commonly used Minor chord.

PARALLEL MINOR CHORDS

It is possible to change the I, IV, and V chords (Illustration 2) to Minor chords. This is accomplished by lowering the third of each triad making each a Minor chord. When these three Major chords are changed to Minor chords they are called PARALLEL MINOR chords.

RELATIVE MINOR CHORDS

ILLUSTRATION **1**

KEY OF C

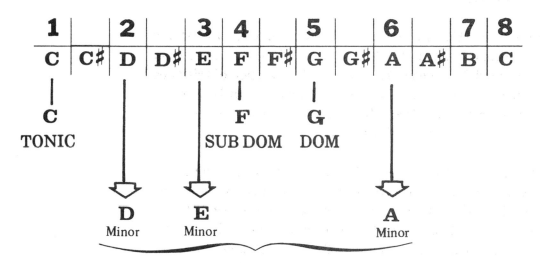

RELATIVE MINOR CHORDS TO THE KEY OF C

ILLUSTRATION **2**

PARALLEL MINOR CHORDS

The 3 primary chords of each key may also be played as minor chords.

EXAMPLE: KEY OF C

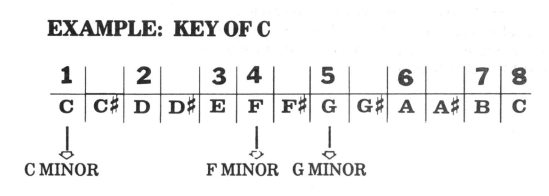

TETRACHORDS

The Major Diatonic Scale is a succession of eight tones arranged in whole steps and half steps. The half steps occurring between the third and fourth, and the seventh and eighth tones of the scale. The first four tones of the scale are called the "First Tetrachord" while the fifth, sixth, seventh, and eighth tones of the scale are called the "Second Tetrachord". Each tetrachord consists of two and one half steps. The two tetrachords are separated by a whole step between the fourth and fifth tones (Illustration 1).

It should be noted that the sharps always occur in the second tetrachord of each scale, while the flats will occur in the first tetrachord. Each tetrachord belongs to two different scales. Each time a new tetrachord is added, a new scale is formed (Illustration 2). Notice in the example given how the upper tetrachord of one scale becomes the lower tetrachord of the following scale (Illustrations 2A, B, C).

CYCLE OF KEYS

If we would continue writing each tetrachord as shown in Illustration 2, we would progress naturally through what is called the CYCLE OF KEYS, returning to the Key of C Major (Illustration 3).

Illustration three shows the Cycle of Keys written in the more familiar arrangement known as the CIRCLE OF FIFTHS. This is discussed on the following page and should be studied as the Circle of Fifths is the basis of modern chord progressions.

ILLUSTRATION 1
THE TETRACHORD

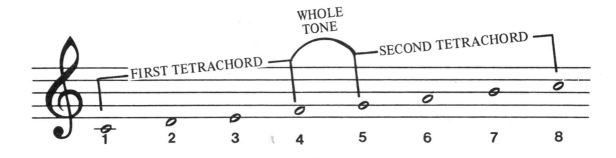

The above chart shows how a major scale is comprised of two tetrachords, each separated by a whole tone.

ILLUSTRATION 2

OVERLAPPING TETRACHORD SCALES

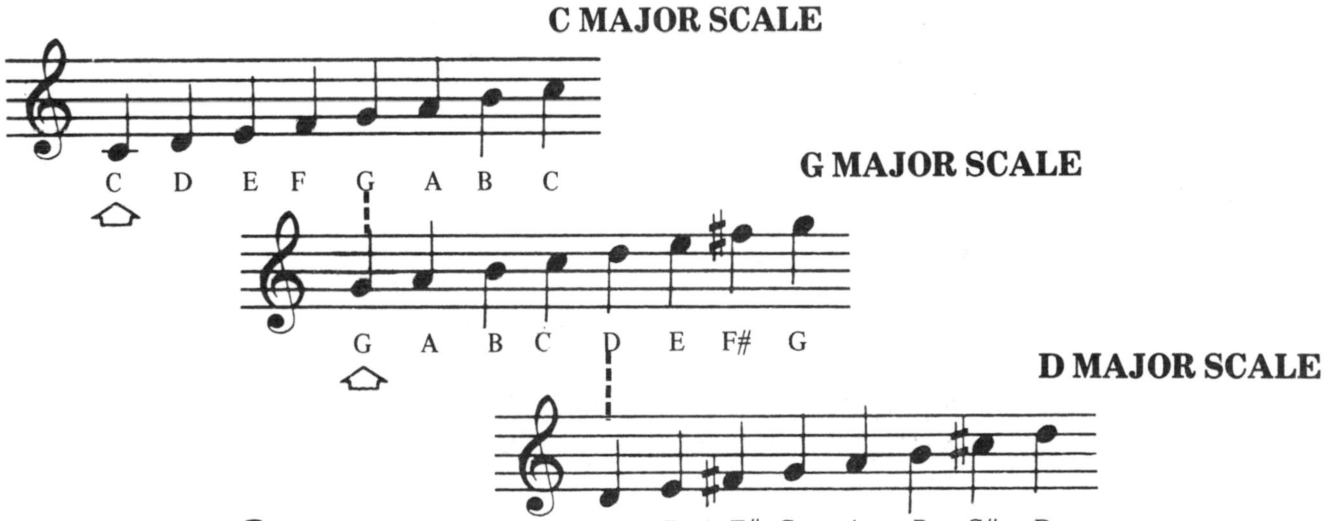

C MAJOR SCALE

C D E F G A B C

G MAJOR SCALE

G A B C D E F# G

D MAJOR SCALE

D E F# G A B C# D

ILLUSTRATION 3
THE CYCLE OF KEYS
(THE CIRCLE OF FIFTHS)

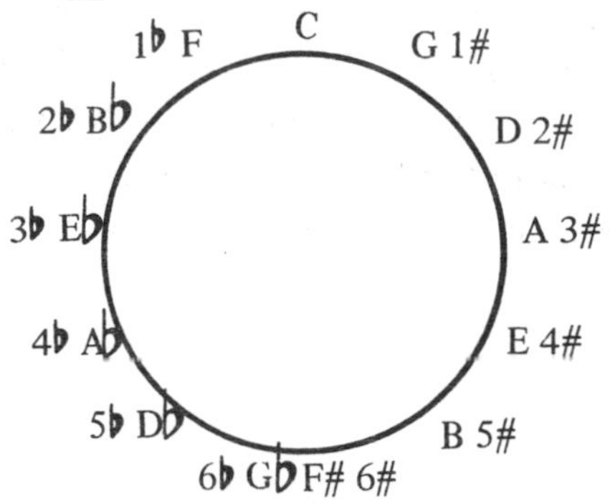

C
1♭ F   G 1#
2♭ B♭   D 2#
3♭ E♭   A 3#
4♭ A♭   E 4#
5♭ D♭   B 5#
6♭ G♭ F# 6#

BASIC CHORD THEORY

THE CIRCLE OF FIFTHS

Guitarists are continually being confronted with new and sometimes bewildering chord progressions. Most all of us at some time have wondered why chords follow such odd patterns. Chords normally do not progress alphabetically: *A B C D E*, etc., instead they skip through the alphabet: *C G D A*, etc. If the student has studied the previous material in this book, the basic principals of harmony as used in chord progressions will have been explained. However, there is one simple tool we need to enable us to better understand chord progressions—THE CIRCLE OF FIFTHS.

For some two hundred years musicians have known that by playing Dominant chords, one can move through all the Keys, progressing in a predictable chord pattern that is pleasant to the ear.

The basic and strongest chord resolution (Progression) in Western world music is the Dominant chord to the Tonic chord. Since each Tonic chord may be thought of as a Dominant chord of some other Key, the progression is endless.

To illustrate this natural progression of fifths (Illustration 1), we start with the *C* Major Diatonic Scale (Illustration 2A). The Tonic chord is *C* Major. Counting up to the 5th degree of the scale, our Dominant chord is *G*. This is the first movement in 5ths. To continue our 5th movement, we make *G* Major our new KEY (Illustration 2B). Our new Tonic chord is *G* Major and the Dominant chord a 5th up is *D*.

Continuing our circle of fifths (Illustration 2C), we make *D* our new key, with *D* Major our new Tonic chord and our new Dominant chord is *A*. This progression can continue until we eventually return to our original chord, *C* Major.

FINDING THE 3 PRIMARY CHORDS TO EACH KEY

If we chose any chord around the circle and make it our Key (Tonic) chord, and then take the chords on either side of it, we would have the three primary chords to the Key or first chord chosen (Illustration 3). We chose the Key of *C*, the *C* Tonic chord. The Dominant chord in the Key of *C* Major is the chord *G* shown to the right of *C* and the Subdominant chord is the chord on the left of *C*, the *F* chord. If we chose the Key of *G* Major, the three primary chords would be: *G* Tonic, *C* Subdominant, and *D* Dominant.

WITH RELATED MINOR CHORDS

Illustration four shows the related Minor chords to each Major chord. The related Minor chord is directly below the Major chords on the inner circle. By utilizing the CIRCLE OF FIFTHS you can easily find six basic chords to any Key.

In the example shown (Illustration 4), the Key of *C* Major, the three primary chords are: *C*, *F*, and *G*. The related Minor chords are *Dm*, *Am*, and *Em*, as shown directly below the Major chords.

THE CIRCLE OF FIFTHS

ILLUSTRATION 1

THE CIRCLE OF FIFTHS

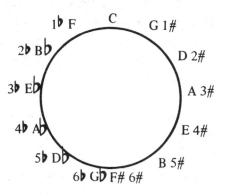

ILLUSTRATION 2

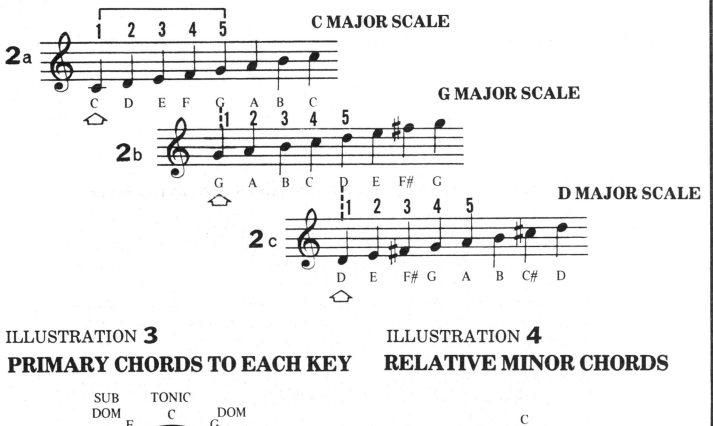

C MAJOR SCALE

2a

C D E F G A B C

G MAJOR SCALE

2b

G A B C D E F# G

D MAJOR SCALE

2c

D E F# G A B C# D

ILLUSTRATION 3

PRIMARY CHORDS TO EACH KEY

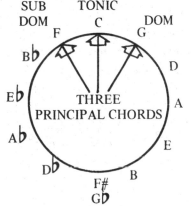

ILLUSTRATION 4

RELATIVE MINOR CHORDS

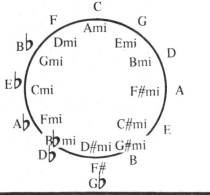

BASIC CHORD THEORY

FORMULAS FOR BUILDING CHORDS

On the following page we present chord formulas. All chord formulas will be under one of five headings denoted by chord types. They are: MAJOR chords, MINOR chords, DOMINANT chords, DIMINISHED chords, and AUGMENTED chords.

We show the chord symbol (alphabetical name), and chord type, extended note. We have used the *C* scale and all chords shown are *C* type chords, however by applying these formulas to any Diatonic Scale you can build any letter name chord desired.

EXAMPLE

We have included seven of the more common Diatonic Scales (KEYS). To build an *F* type chord, apply the proper formula to the *F* Diatonic Scale. To find the proper notes to build a *G* type chord, apply the correct formula for the desired chord to the *G* Diatonic Scale.

HOW TO TRANSPOSE

By using the Diatonic Scales as presented, it is possible to transpose chords from one KEY to another. To transpose the chords of a song to another Key—FIRST, determine the Key the song is written or played in. Once the Key has been established, utilize the Diatonic Scale of that letter name and locate each chord by number. Example: If the song were written in the Key of *F* and the chord progression were as follows— *F*, *B♭*, *F*, *Gmi*, *Ami6*, *B♭*, *C7*, *F*, checking the *F* Diatonic Scale we find these eight chords under the following numbers: 1, 4, 1, 2, 3, 4, 5, 1. To transpose this song to the Key of *G*, simply use the *G* Diatonic Scale and look under these numbers to find the new chords. The new chord progression would now be— *G*, *C*, *G*, *Ami*, *Bmi6*, *C*, *D7*, *G*.

When transposing chords we change only the letter name, we do not change the chord type. The minor chords (the *G* minor) and the extended minor chord remain. The new chords are *Ami* and *Bmi6*. Should there be a Diminished or Augmented chord be sure to play the new chords that way.

FORMULAS FOR BUILDING CHORDS

CHORD	FORMULA	CHORD SYMBOL
MAJOR		
MAJOR CHORD	1 3 5	C
MAJOR SIXTH	1 3 5 6	C6, C Maj. 6
MAJOR SIXTH, ADD NINE	1 3 5 6 9	C6 add 9
MAJOR SEVENTH	1 3 5 7	C Maj. 7
MAJOR NINTH	1 3 5 7 9	CM9, C Maj. 9
MINOR		
MINOR CHORD	1 ♭3 5	Cm, C min.
MINOR SIXTH	1 ♭3 5 6	Cm6, C min. 6
MINOR SEVENTH	1 ♭3 5 ♭7	Cm7, C min. 7
MINOR SEVEN, FLAT FIVE	1 ♭3 ♭5 ♭7	Cm7♭5
MINOR NINTH	1 ♭3 5 ♭7 9	Cm9, C min. 9
DOMINANT		
DOMINANT SEVENTH	1 3 5 ♭7	C7
DOMINANT SEVEN ♭5	1 3 ♭5 ♭7	C7♭5
DOMINANT SEVENTH, ♭9	1 3 5 ♭7 ♭9	C7♭9
DOMINANT SEVENTH #9	1 3 5 ♭7 #9	C7#9
DOMINANT SEVENTH, SUS	1 #3 5 ♭7	C7 sus 4
DOMINANT NINTH	1 3 5 ♭7 9	C9
DOMINANT THIRTEENTH	1 3 5 ♭7 9 13	C 13 (*C9add6*)
DIMINISHED		
DIMINISHED CHORD	1 ♭3 ♭5 6 (♭♭7)	C dim. 7, C—, C°
AUGMENTED		
AUGMENTED CHORD	1 3 #5	C Aug., C+
AUGMENTED SEVENTH	1 3 #5 ♭7	C7Aug., C7+5

KEY OF A

1	2	3	4	5	6	7	8
A	B	C#	D	E	F#	G#	A

KEY OF B♭

1	2	3	4	5	6	7	8
B♭	C	D	E♭	F	G	A	B♭

KEY OF C

1	2	3	4	5	6	7	8
C	D	E	F	G	A	B	C

KEY OF D

1	2	3	4	5	6	7	8
D	E	F#	G	A	B	C#	D

KEY OF E

1	2	3	4	5	6	7	8
E	F#	G#	A	B	C#	D#	E

KEY OF F

1	2	3	4	5	6	7	8
F	G	A	B♭	C	D	E	F

KEY OF G

1	2	3	4	5	6	7	8
G	A	B	C	D	E	F#	G

·HOW TO PLAY CHORDS

·WHAT ARE OPEN STRING CHORDS

·PRIMARY CHORDS TO EACH KEY

In this section we have included many of the more common chords used in today's music. Since these are all the simpler open string chords played within the first three frets, none of the more sophisticated Jazz chords are included. This section is designed for the beginning student and those players who need to familiarize themselves with the chord groupings belonging to each Key.

The chords are arranged in Keys, as this is how they are used. These are the three primary chords that are used in most songs, plus the Minor chords that may occasionally be used.

OPEN STRING CHORDS

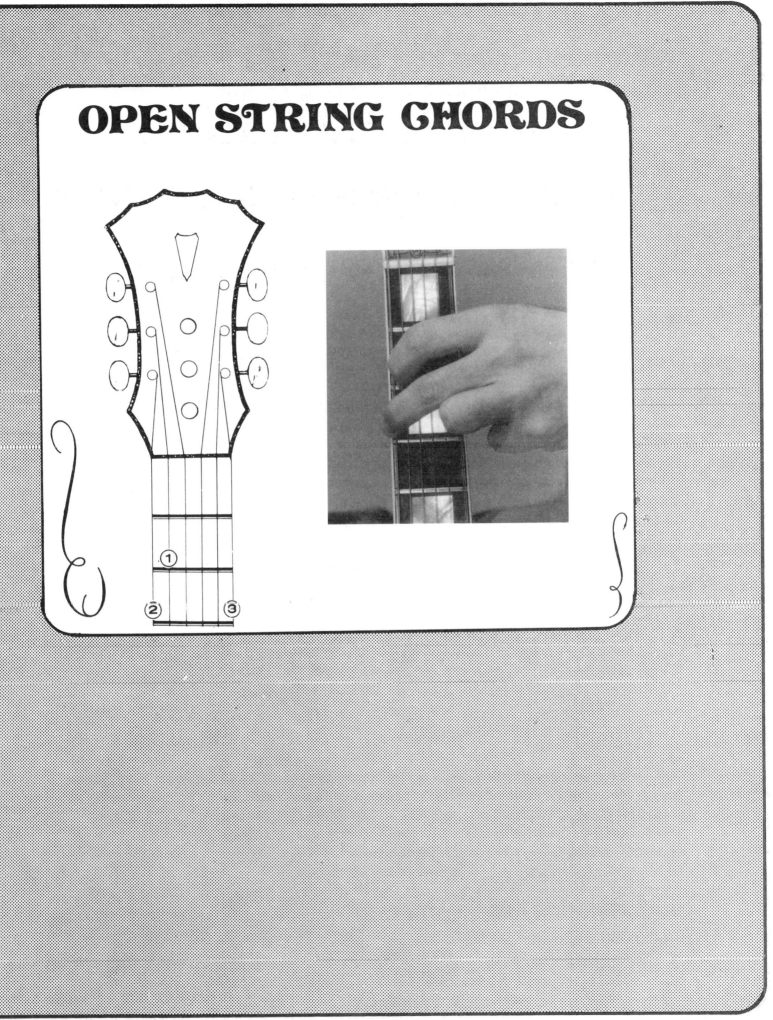

HOW TO READ CHORD DIAGRAMS

The chord diagrams used in this book have been developed to show you where to place your fingers to play each chord. The numbers indicate the proper finger to use on each string and fret. To aid the student in note reading we have included the written arrangement of the chord with the notes arranged in order of their appearance when strumming the guitar. The lowest note is always on the bottom of the stack. The lowest note of the chord is the first note played when you strum.

The numbers for the fingers have been placed in the most practical and complete position for each chord. While there are several different fingerings possible for most of these chords, learn to play them as presented.

Illustration one shows the proper fingering for the *G* chord. Illustration one-b indicates the correct fingering for the chord, and the note sequence is indicated by the written chord next to it. Illustration two-a and two-b indicate the accepted fingering for playing the *C* chord. In Illustration two-b we indicate the fretting of the 5th and 6th strings at the third fret with the third finger. The student should try to develop the ability to do this as it allows the playing of all six strings while freeing the fourth finger to be used in playing other notes such as the B♭ in the C7 chord.

At all times keep the fingers directly behind the frets as indicated in the diagrams. Press firmly to assure all strings will sound properly. If a string buzzes, check the fingering and press harder. Be sure the fingernails are clipped short. To properly fret the strings you must use the ends of the fingers. Until you have developed calluses you will find the strings difficult to fret regardless of what you do. Eliminating this problem requires steady, daily practice. Eventually as the skin on the pads of fingers harden, producing calluses, then you will find it requires less pressure to fret the strings.

When a chord diagram indicates that one finger should fret two strings and you are unable to do so, it is permissible to leave off the lowest sounding tone (Illustration 2b). You could eliminate the 6th string altogether and still have a pleasant sounding chord. If the unfretted string is going to be struck with the pick when strumming, it should be muted or deadened with one of the other fingers.

HOW FINGERS ARE NUMBERED

The illustration at right shows how the fingers on the left hand are numbered. **NOTE:** The thumb is not used in any of these chord fingerings.

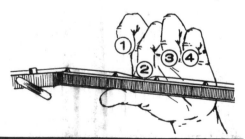

OPEN STRING CHORDS

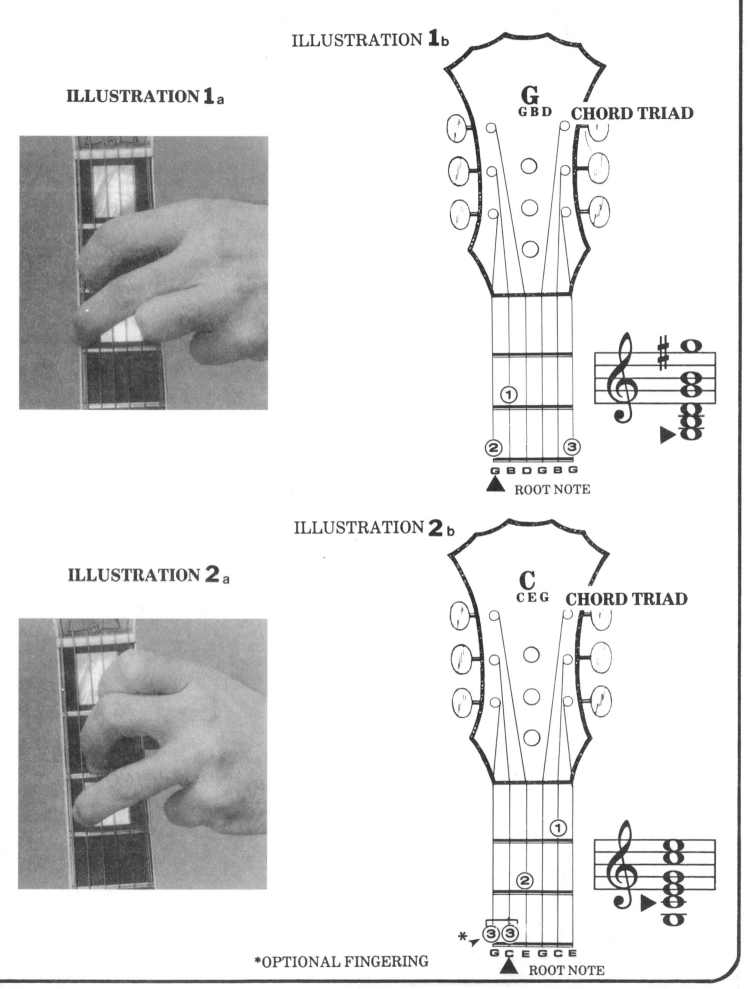

ILLUSTRATION **1**b

ILLUSTRATION **1**a

G
G B D CHORD TRIAD

① ② ③

G B D G B G

▲ ROOT NOTE

ILLUSTRATION **2**b

ILLUSTRATION **2**a

C
C E G CHORD TRIAD

① ②

*⌐ ③③

G C E G C E

*OPTIONAL FINGERING

▲ ROOT NOTE

OPEN STRING CHORDS

OPEN STRING CHORDS

The term "OPEN STRING CHORD" is used to indicate those chords normally played within the first three frets, using strings other than those that are fretted. In Illustration one we show the chord *A* at the second fret. We only fret (finger) three strings, yet we can strum all six strings as indicated. Most all Major and Minor chords can be played in this manner. Chords such as *C, D, E, G, A, B*, etc., utilize some open strings when played within the first three frets on the guitar.

Beyond the 3rd fret it is not possible to play most chords with the customary three fingers using open strings, as the notes of the open string do not conform to the notes of the chord triad.

To understand why we can use "open string" chords the student will need some knowledge of chord construction. Primary knowledge of chord triads is required. Simply stated, a "triad" is the three notes that form each chord. The triad of the *A* chord is—*A C# E*. When these three notes are played together anywhere on the guitar, we have the chord *A* (Illustration 2). We fret three strings as shown in Illustration one. Actually we are fretting the notes *E A* and *C#*, the triad of the *A* chord. However the 6th and 5th and 1st strings are also *A* and *E* notes, notes of the *A* chord triad. Since these open strings are notes of the *A* chord triad we can play them without fretting these notes. The basic rule of chord construction states that we must play at least one of each of the notes of the triad, however we can have multiples of any one of the notes. Also they can be arranged in any order (sequence).

OPEN STRING CHORDS

OPEN STRING CHORD

A

ILLUSTRATION **1**

USING ALL SIX STRINGS

A TRIAD 1 3 5
A C# E

ILLUSTRATION **2**

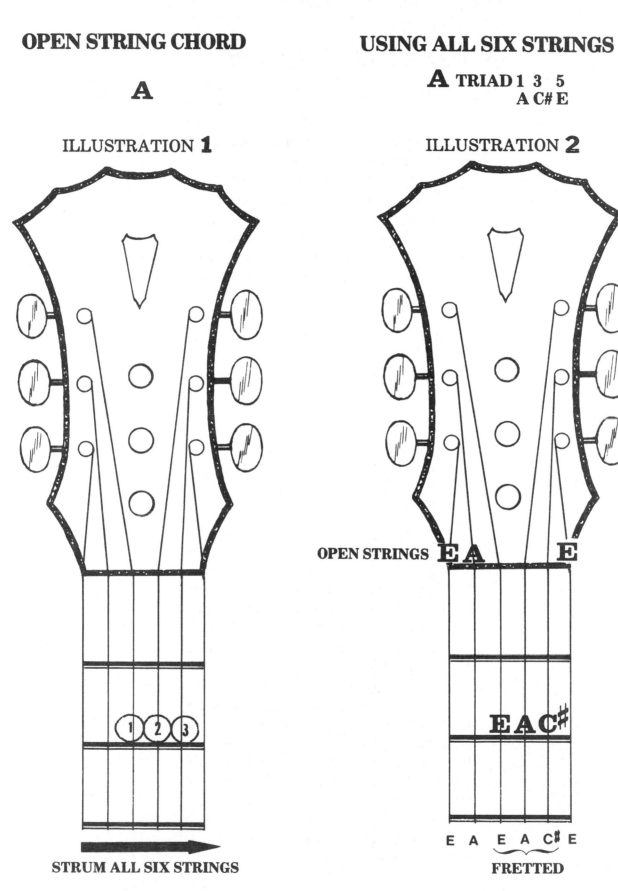

STRUM ALL SIX STRINGS

OPEN STRINGS E A   E

E A C#

E A   E A C# E

FRETTED

OPEN STRING CHORDS
UP THE NECK

We can play the three notes of the chord triad anywhere on the guitar neck. In the section titled "Barr Chords", we discuss this in detail and show how chords can, by INVERSION, be played at various places on the neck. However, there is a simple, little understood, principal that all beginners should become familiar with. This technique utilizes the playing of higher octave fretted notes simultaneously with lower octave open strings.

In Illustration one, we show the familiar *A* chord with the three notes *E A C#* fretted at the 2nd fret. When strumming we also play the open 6th, 5th, and 1st strings adding two more *E* notes and one more *A* note, giving the chord a full six string sound. Remember that we can play these notes anywhere we find them. In Illustration two we show these same three strings fretted at the 5th, 6th, and 7th frets respectively. This again gives us the three necessary notes to produce the *A* chord triad, *A C# E*, however in a different sequence. The note sequence, Illustration one, is *E A E A C# E*, six through the first string. At the fifth fret, Illustration two, strumming all six strings the sequence would be—*E A A C# A E*. In different order, yet still only the three notes of the *A* chord triad. Play this chord, Illustration two, and listen to the open strings beating against the fretted strings—a very unique sound.

This technique can be accomplished with many chords and can be very useful, especially in finger style of playing.

OPEN STRING CHORDS

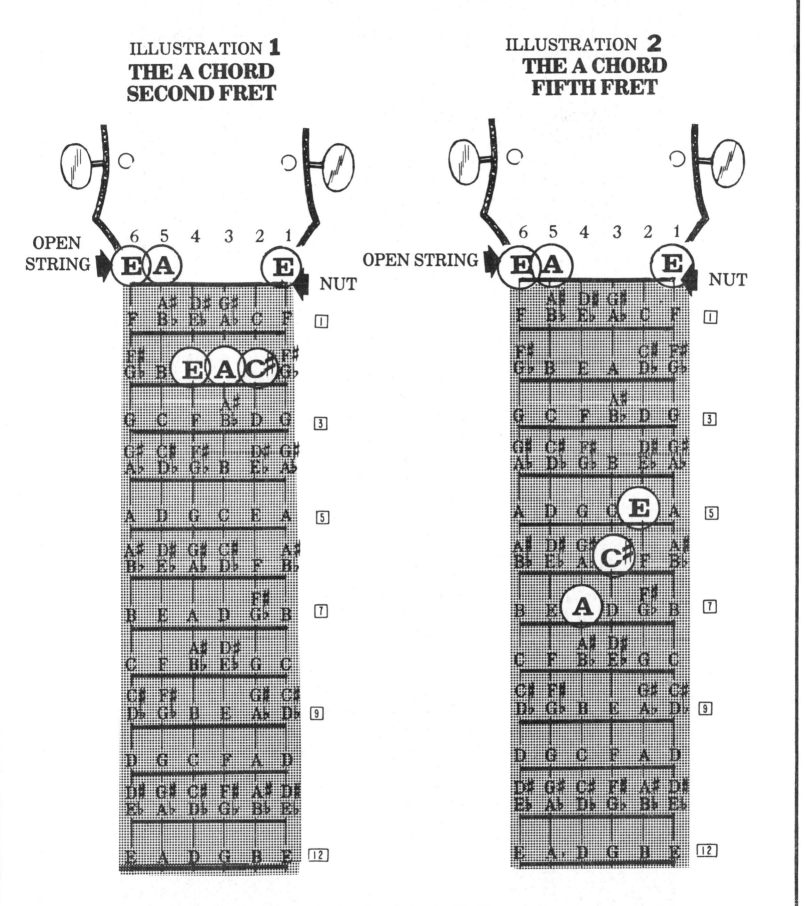

ILLUSTRATION **1**
**THE A CHORD
SECOND FRET**

ILLUSTRATION **2**
**THE A CHORD
FIFTH FRET**

The notes of the *A* chord triad, *A C# E*, may be played at any position and in any order on the guitar neck.

OPEN STRING CHORDS

THE B7 POSITION

The *B7* chord (Illustration 1) is a very interesting chord form. In Country music it can be used to create special song endings we have all heard. The *B7* chord triad is: *B Eb Gb* and *A*. The open second, *B* string, can be used in playing this chord. If we slide this chord position up one fret the Root note becomes *C* and at this fret the chord becomes a *C7* chord. Actually it is both a Dominant 7 type chord and a Major 7 type. The note added to the triad at this position to make it a Dominant 7 chord is the note *Bb*. We also have the seventh note of the *C* Scale, the note *B*, open second string. Normally this is not good practice as there is a dissonant sound created. If this chord form is used at this fret, it must be used as a "Passing Tone", and must be a quick movement in a moving chord progression.

When the *B7* chord form is moved up one more fret, placing the Root note on the fourth fret, Illustration three, we have a *C#7*, and again the open *B* string can be utilized as the note *B* is a note of the *C#7* chord triad.

In Illustration four, we have this chord form moved up to the 7th fret making it an *E7* chord, and again utilizing the open *B* string as part of the chord triad. This position of the *E* chord can be used quite successfully in conjunction with the three string *A* chord as shown on the previous page.

HOW TO USE THE B7 POSITION

The three primary chords in the Key of *E* are: *E A* and *B7*. When playing in this Key we can create a very pleasant chord progression using this chord form as a *C#7*, *C7* and *B7*. Practice playing this progression. Note the number of beats each chord receives, the slanted lines receive one beat each. The first and last *E* should be the open string first position as shown on page **74**. Use the *E7* (Illustration 4) in the third measure. Another good chord progression can be developed as a song ending by simply playing this progression and playing only the first and third string, eliminating the other strings. Try It!

OPEN STRING CHORDS

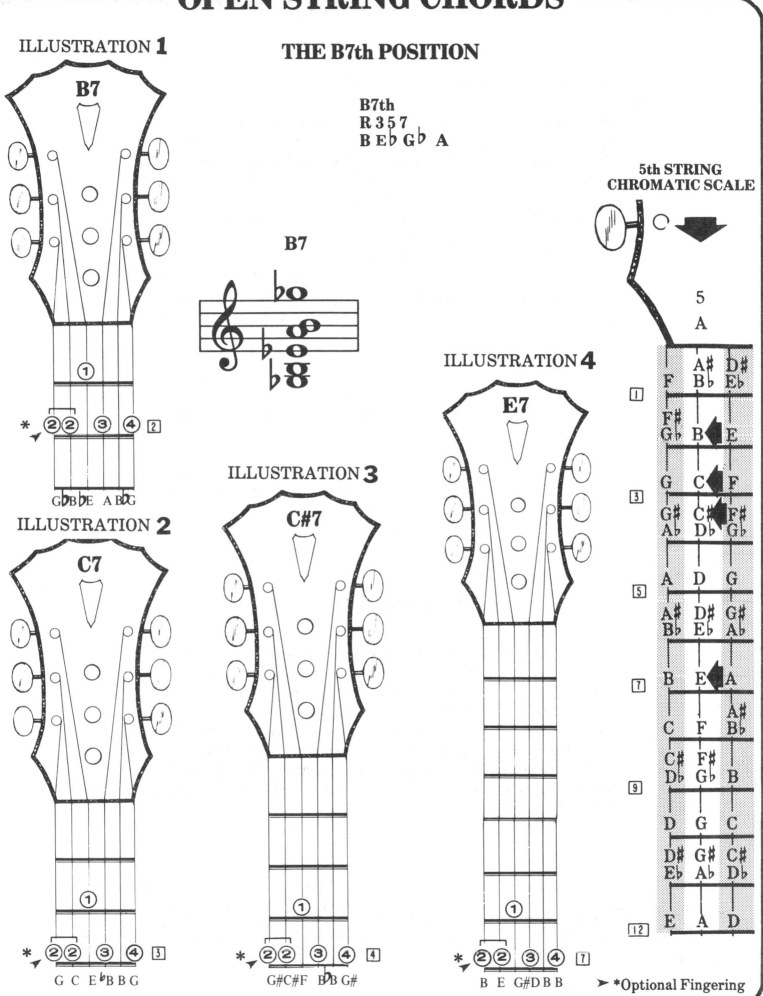

ILLUSTRATION **1**

B7

THE B7th POSITION

B7th
R 3 5 7
B E♭ G♭ A

B7

5th STRING
CHROMATIC SCALE

5
A

* ②② ③ ④ [2]

G♭ B♭ D♭ E A B♭ G

ILLUSTRATION **2**

C7

ILLUSTRATION **3**

C#7

ILLUSTRATION **4**

E7

* ②② ③ ④ [3]

G C E♭ B♭ B G

* ②② ③ ④ [4]

G#C#F B♭ B G#

* ②② ③ ④ [7]

B E G#D B B

➤ *Optional Fingering

F	A# B♭	D# E♭
F# G♭	B	E
G	C	F
G# A♭	C# D♭	F# G♭
A	D	G
A# B♭	D# E♭	G# A♭
B	E	A
C	F	A# B♭
C# D♭	F# G♭	B
D	G	C
D# E♭	G# A♭	C# D♭
E	A	D

OPEN STRING CHORDS

BASIC CHORD CHART

On the following pages we present a BASIC CHORD CHART, showing one fingering for SEVEN chords of each letter name. (Example: *C, C6, C7, Cmi, Cmaj7, Cdim, Caug.*).

These have been prepared for most of the more commonly used Keys. We do not show most of the flat keys as they require difficult fingering for most "Open String" chord forms.

ADDITIONAL CHORDS

On page 75, we also present one form of the 9th chord for each alphabetical name. There are many different fingerings possible for all these chords, however we show only one of the more common forms.

PRIMARY CHORDS TO ALL KEYS

On the following pages we have presented the three primary chords—the TONIC, SUB DOMINANT and DOMINANT chords, plus the two more common MINOR chords for most of the more frequently used Keys.

You should learn chords by these Key groupings. This is essential if you wish to play by ear. There are many more chords that may be used, however these five chords appear most frequently.

BASIC CHORD CHART

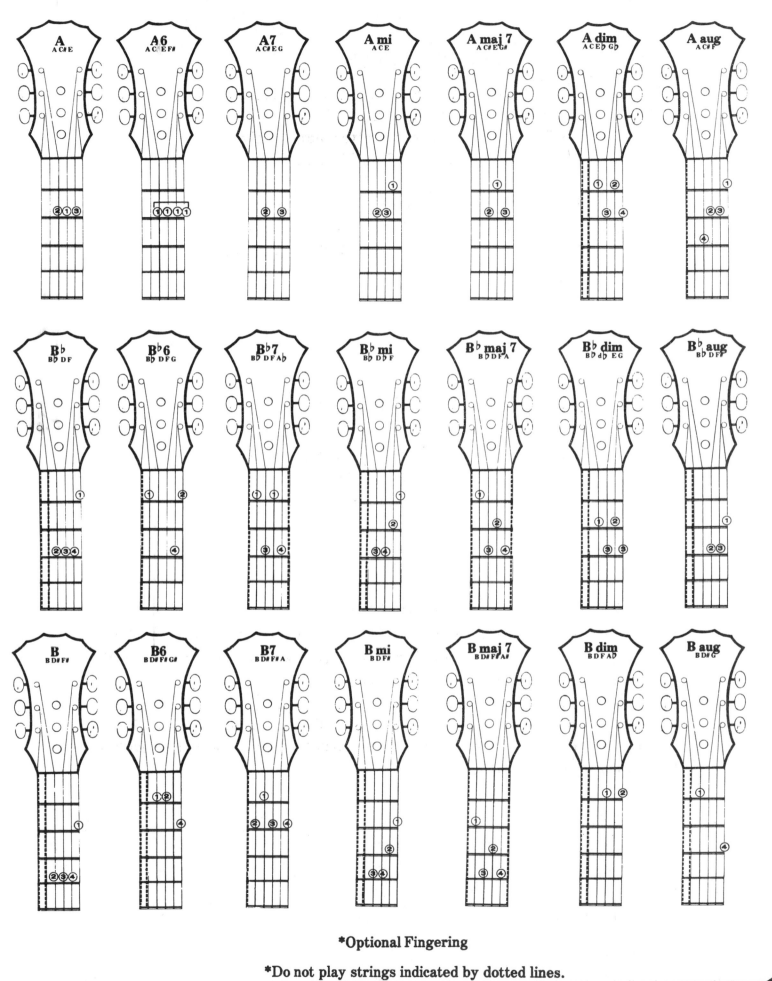

*Optional Fingering

*Do not play strings indicated by dotted lines.

BASIC CHORD CHART

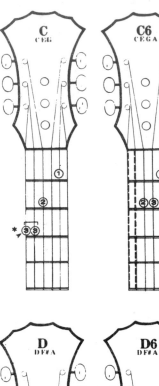
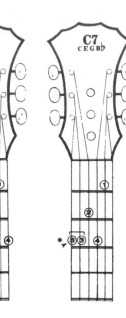
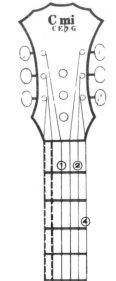

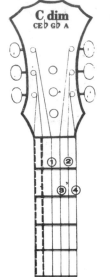

C
C E G

C6
C E G A

C7
C E G B♭

C mi
C E♭ G

C maj 7
C E G B

C dim
C E♭ G♭ A

C aug
C E G♯

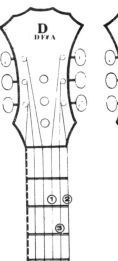
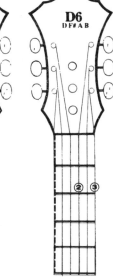

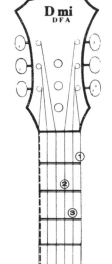
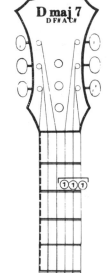
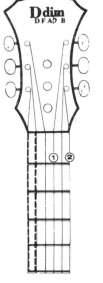
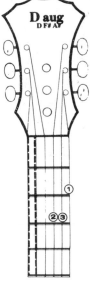

D
D F♯ A

D6
D F♯ A B

D7
D F♯ A C

D mi
D F A

D maj 7
D F♯ A C♯

D dim
D F A♭ B

D aug
D F♯ A♯

E
E G♯ B

E6
E G♯ B C♯

E7
E G♯ B D

E mi
E G B

E maj 7
E G♯ B D♯

E dim
E G B♭ D

E aug
E G C

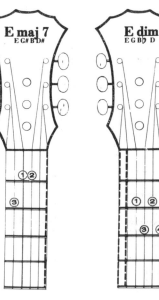

*Optional Fingering

*Do not play strings indicated by dotted lines.

74

BASIC CHORD CHART

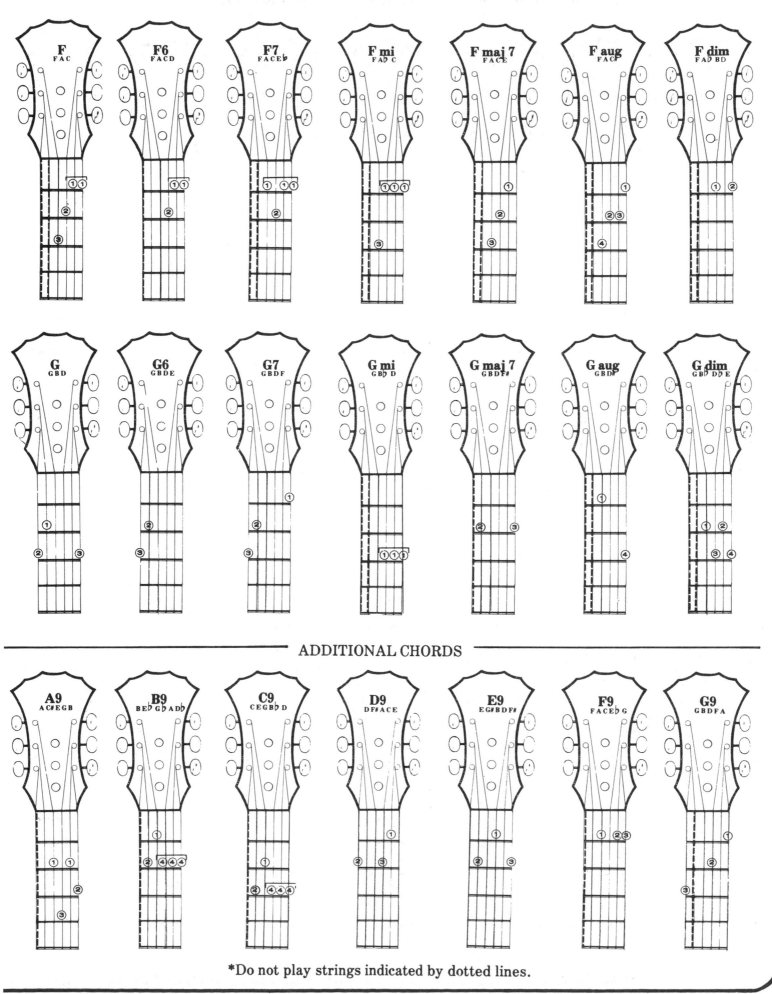

ADDITIONAL CHORDS

*Do not play strings indicated by dotted lines.

75

KEY OF A

*Do not play strings indicated by dotted lines.

TONIC

A
A C# E

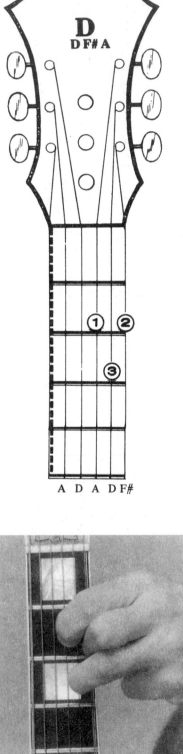

E A E A C# E

SUB DOM

D
D F# A

A D A D F#

DOM 7

E7
E B G# D

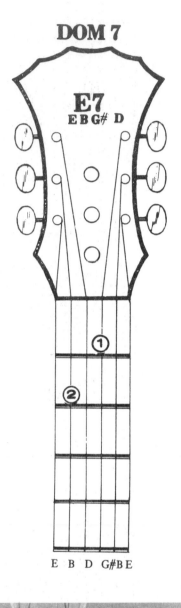

E B D G# B E

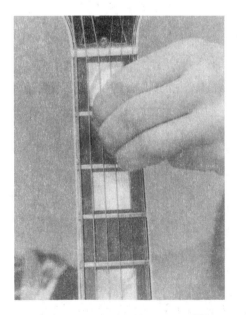
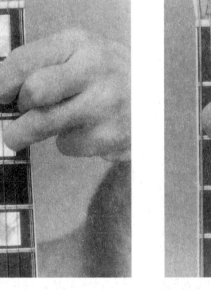
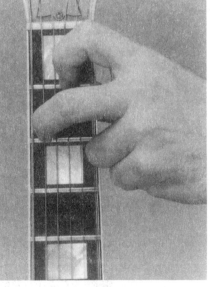

*Do not play strings indicated by dotted lines.

TONIC

D
DF#A

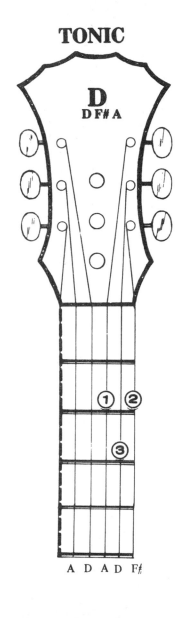

A D A D F#

SUB DOM

G
GBD

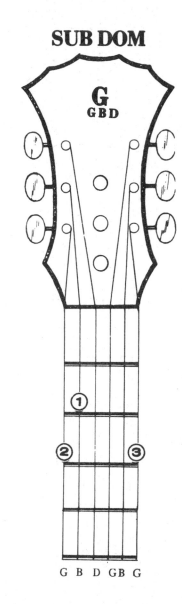

G B D GB G

DOM 7

A7
AC#EG

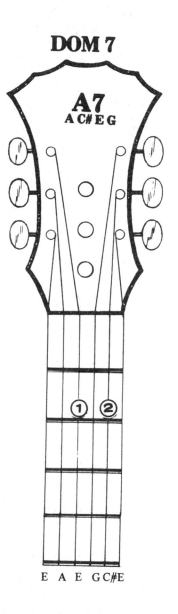

E A E GC#E

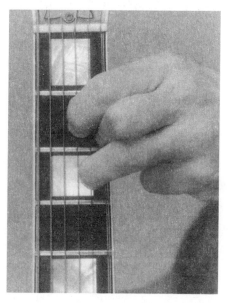

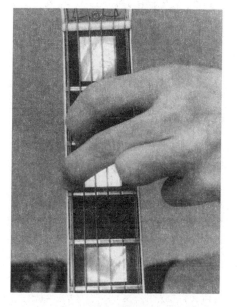

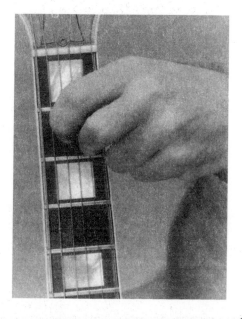

KEY OF C

TONIC

SUB DOM

DOM 7

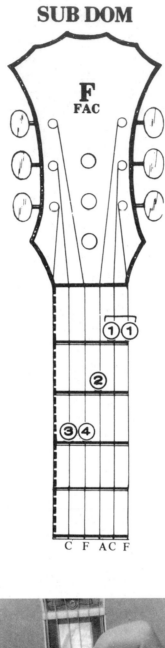

C
C E G

G C E G C E

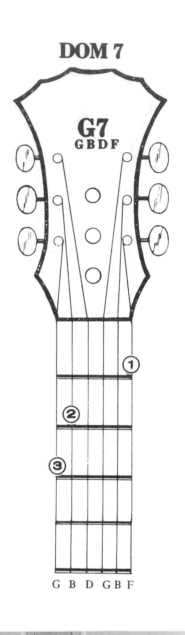

F
F A C

C F A C F

G7
G B D F

G B D G B F

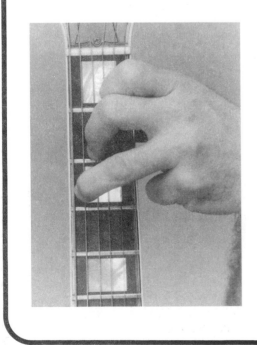

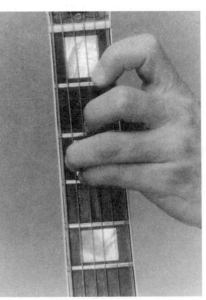

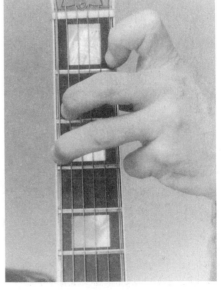

78

TONIC

SUB DOM

DOM 7

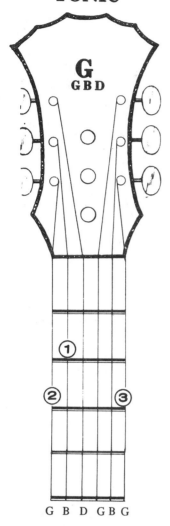

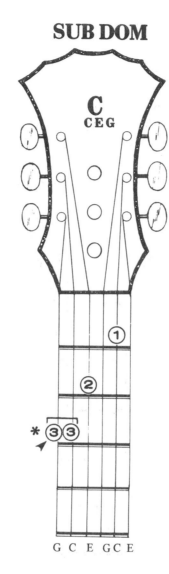

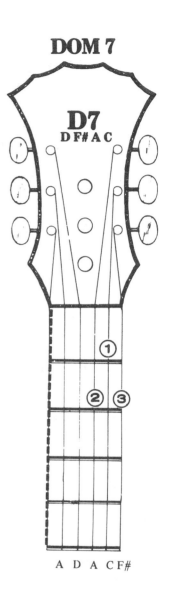

G B D G B G

G C E G C E

A D A C F#

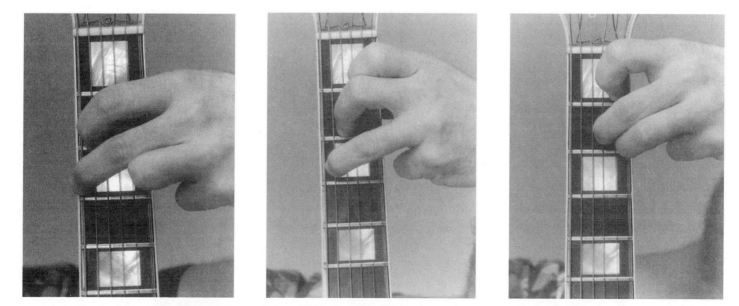

*Optional Fingering   Do not play strings indicated by dotted lines.

KEY OF E

TONIC	SUB DOM	DOM 7

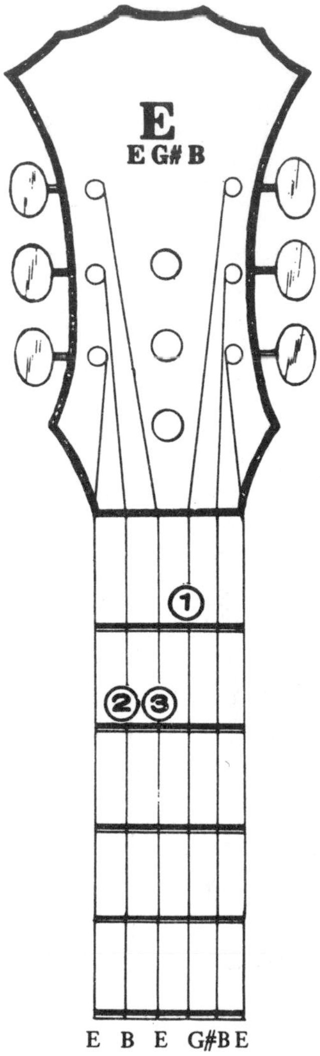

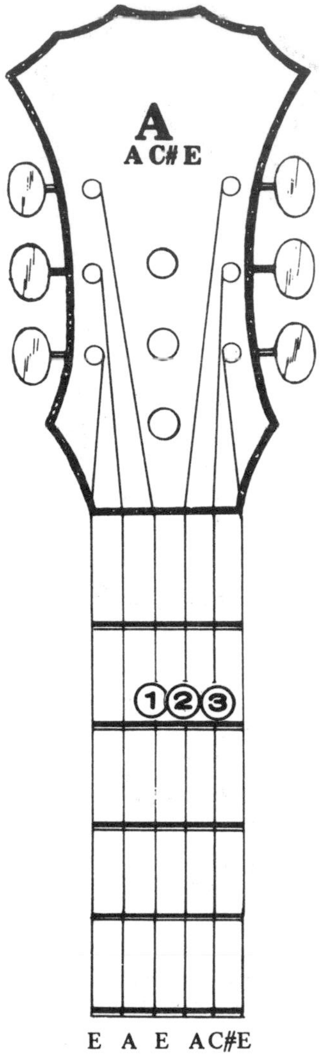

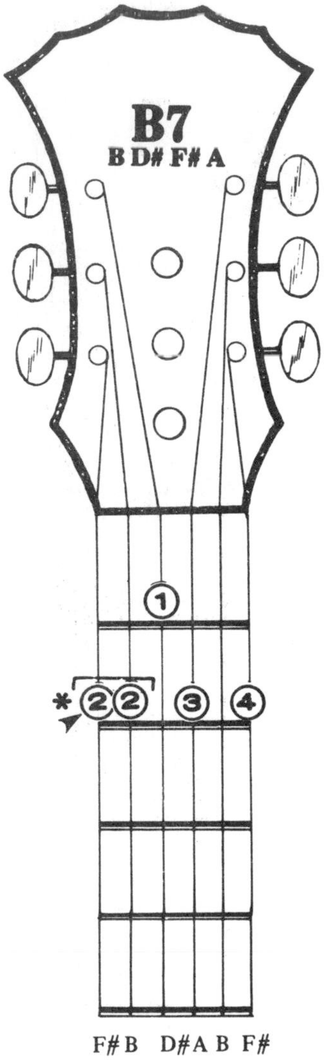

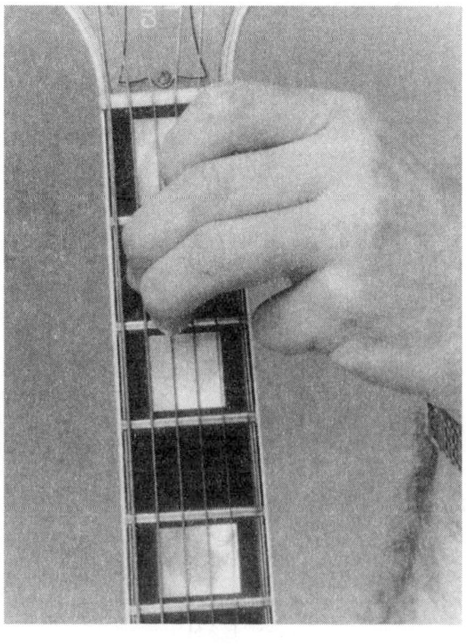

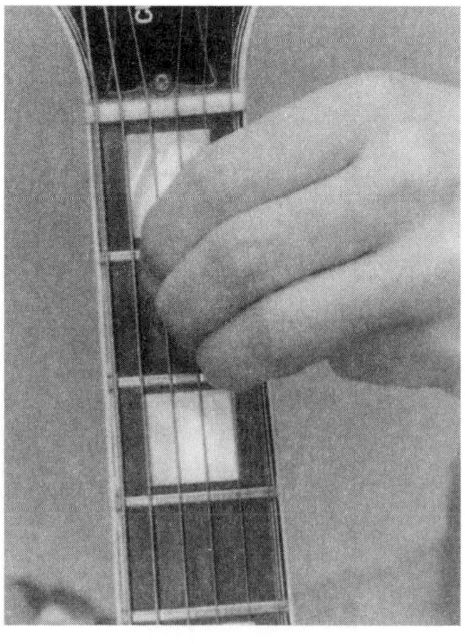

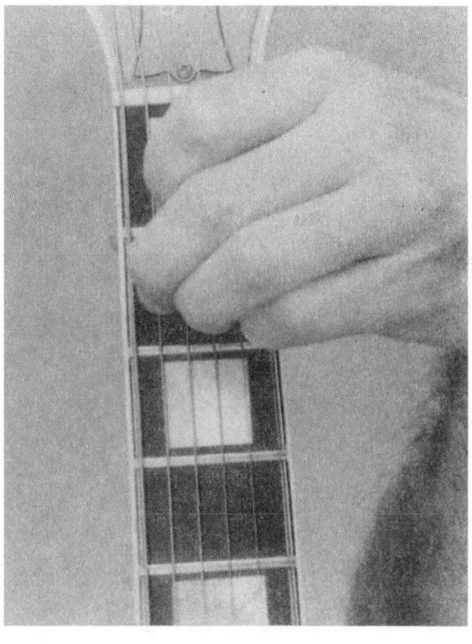

E
E G# B

A
A C# E

B7
B D# F# A

E   B   E   G#B E

E   A   E   AC#E

F#B   D#A B   F#

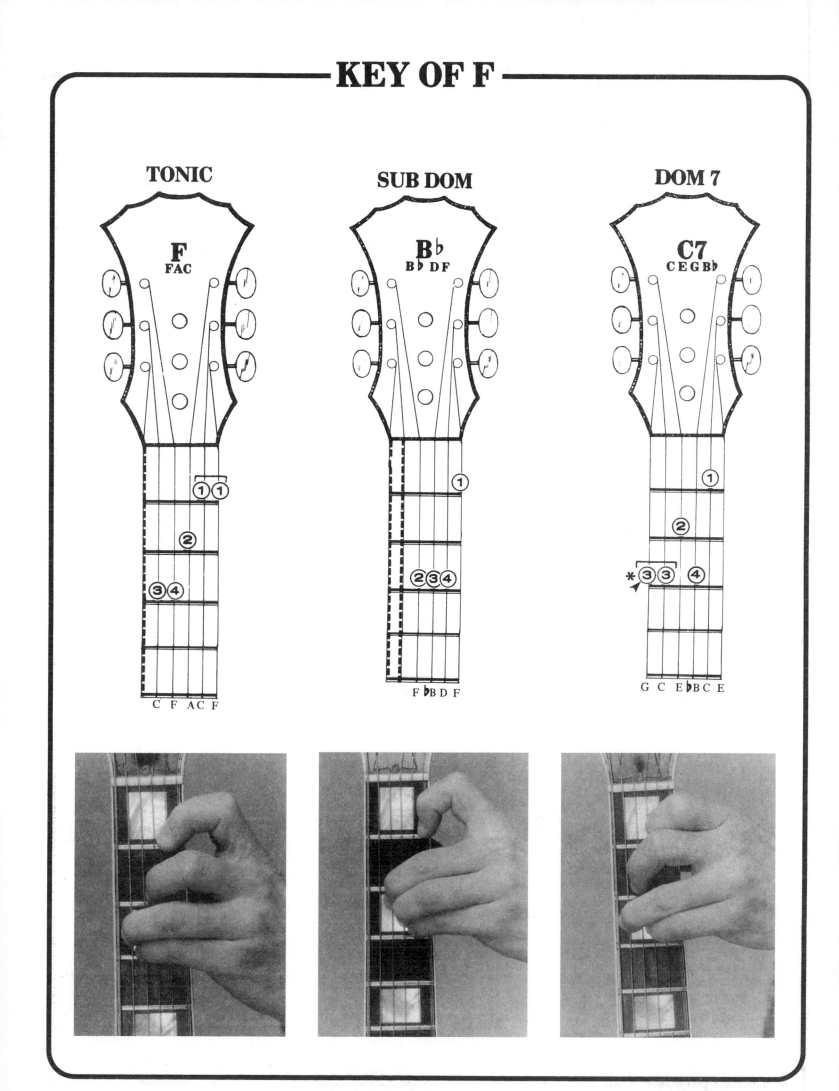

TONIC

SUB DOM

DOM 7

F
FAC

B♭
B♭ D F

C7
C E G B♭

C F AC F

F ♭B D F

G C E♭B C E

PRIMARY CHORDS TO ALL KEYS

KEY OF B♭

TONIC	SUB DOM	DOM 7

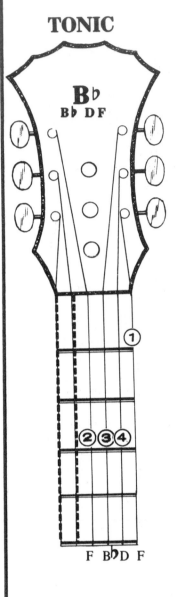

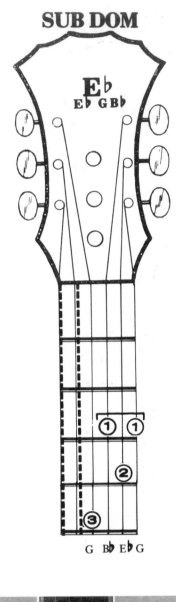

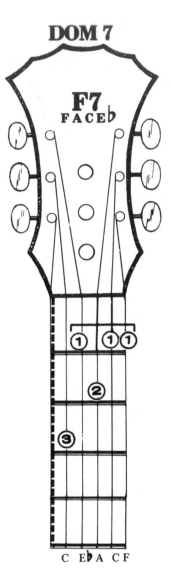

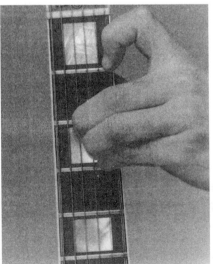

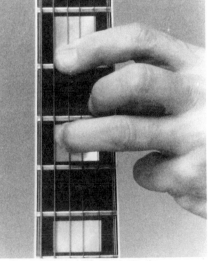

*Do not play strings indicated by dotted lines.

PRIMARY CHORDS TO ALL KEYS

KEY OF E♭

TONIC

E♭
E♭ G B♭

G B♭ E♭ G

SUB DOM

A♭
A♭ C E♭

E♭ A♭ C A♭

DOM 7

B♭7
B♭ D F A♭

E♭ F A♭ D F

*Do not play strings indicated by dotted lines.

THREE FORMS

276 CHORDS

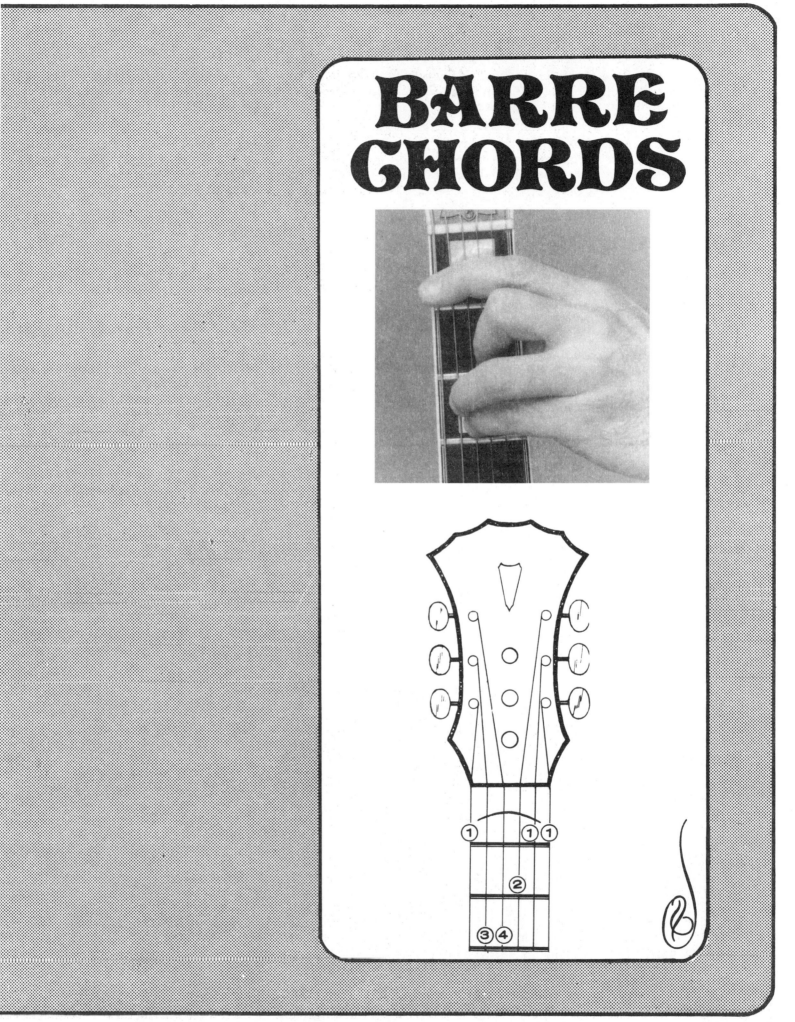

BARRE CHORDS

BARRE CHORDS

Without the knowledge of the Barre chords we would not be able to play chords beyond the first three frets, and it would be very difficult to play rhythm in some Keys. Actually the Barre chords are nothing more than the three fingered open string chords moved up the neck. This is accomplished by substituting our first finger for the "NUT" of the guitar, in effect shortening the neck at the fret the finger is barred across.

By barring across the neck we make the chords "MOVABLE". They can be moved up or down the neck, becoming a new chord at each fret. Playing Barre chords can be quite difficult, and will require a great deal of practice. However, with practice Barre chords will be as easy to play as the open string three finger chords.

DOING IT RIGHT

To successfully play Barre chords the student must first be sure he understands what he is playing, and secondly, be sure he is playing it properly. At first the extra strain on the left hand, wrist and forearm may seem unbearable. However with practice you will be able to play them with ease.

If you are just starting to learn Barre chords follow the procedures outlined in this book, and practice playing Barre chords daily. Only a determined effort on your part will resolve the difficulties that may arise.

There are several things the student should be aware of to eliminate unnecessary problems. First, the first finger must be used to make the Barre, however it is not necessary for it to fret all six strings. Observe Illustration Two. We use the second, third and fourth fingers to form the basic chord. The Barre finger is used to fret only those strings left unfretted, the 1st, 2nd, and the 6th strings. It is not necessary for the first finger to hold down all six strings. Slightly curving the first fingers over the 3rd, 4th, and 5th strings will ease the strain on the left wrist. Secondly, by keeping the wrist bent and the fingers arched, playing on the fingertips, will make it easier to obtain a clear sound without string buzz. Third, if you have a dead string, or one that buzzes when played, observe which string is at fault. If it is one being fretted by the second, third, or first finger, increasing pressure on the first (Barre) finger will not eliminate the problem and only tire the arm and wrist. Check your left hand thumb position. It should be well underneath the neck of the instrument.

KEEP LEFT WRIST BENT AND ELBOW OUT FROM BODY

Proper left hand technique is very necessary as it eliminates undue strain, and will also place the fingers in position to play additional notes. Keep the wrist bent and keep the palms of the hand away from the neck. While the first finger must, necessarily be fairly flat, try to keep the other fingers arched and play on the ends of the fingers. Be sure your fingernails are clipped short. Another common fault is keeping the elbow in toward the body. This practice tends to pull the wrist out straight and adds to the difficulty in getting a good Barre with the first finger. Keep the elbow out and down under the neck.

THE GRAND BARRE   ROOT POSITION

The Barre chord (Illustration 3) is the most useful and the most commonly used of the three Barre chords presented in this section. It is also the easiest to learn. It is formally called the "Grand Barre". In modern terms it is called: Bar or Barre chord.

We begin by first placing the fingers in position to play the *E* chord (Illustration 1).

ALTERNATE FINGERING

We must free the first finger in order to use it for the Barre (Illustration 2). Substitute the second, third and fourth fingers to form the *E* chord as shown. Keep the first finger free.

MOVABLE "BARRE" CHORD

Slide your hand down a few frets, keeping your fingers in position. Then place your first finger across the neck, fretting the 6th string with the end of the finger. Fret the first and second string with the upper part of the finger. Should you have difficulty obtaining a clear sound on all six strings, check and see which finger is at fault. Sometimes a string will be under a wrinkle in the first finger, and you may need to slightly readjust the position of the first finger to eliminate this condition.

FORM ONE "ROOT" POSITION

THE "GRAND BARRE" BASE POSITION, THE E MAJOR CHORD

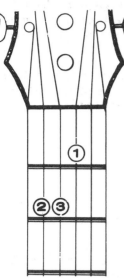

ILLUSTRATION **1**

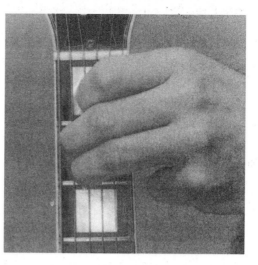

NOW SUBSTITUTE ALTERNATE FINGERING

ILLUSTRATION **2**

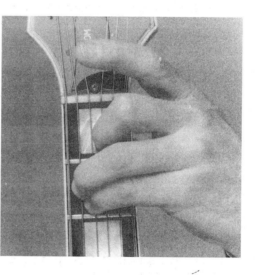

THE MOVABLE "BARRE" CHORD

ILLUSTRATION **3**

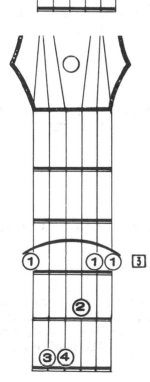

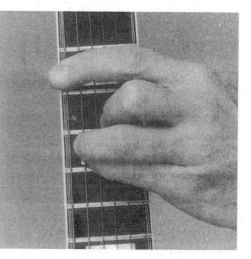

THE ROOT POSITION

The *F* Barre chord is actually the *E* chord moved one fret up the neck and the bar finger added in substitution for the "Nut". Each chord derives its name from the Root note of its triad. In this first form of the Barre chord the Root name will always be on the 6th string. Whichever note is fretted by the Barre finger on the sixth string will be the name of the chord.

All diagrams will show which fingers to use to fret each chord (Illustration 1). The chord in written form, showing each note as it is actually fretted on the guitar is included.

We have provided both the horizontal Diatonic Scale, Illustration Four A, and the written Diatonic scale with the triad marked, Illustration Four B, to aid you to better understanding of the concepts being taught.

FORM ONE "ROOT" POSITION

ILLUSTRATION 1

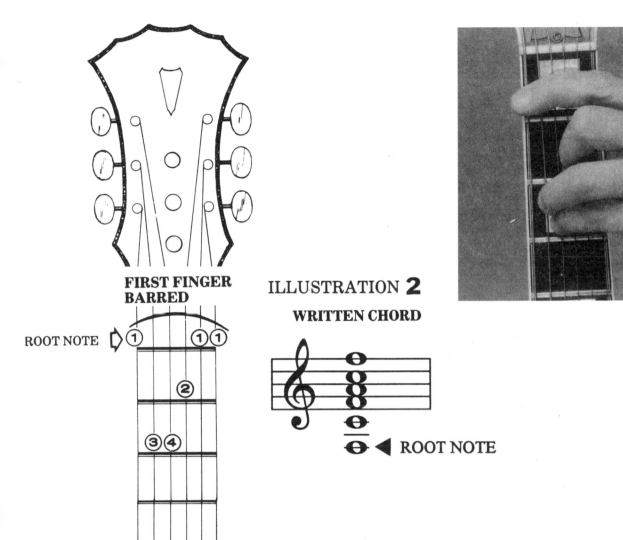

FIRST FINGER BARRED

ROOT NOTE

F C F A C F

ILLUSTRATION 2

WRITTEN CHORD

◄ ROOT NOTE

ILLUSTRATION 3

ILLUSTRATION 4 a

DIATONIC SCALE

1	2	3	4	5	6	7	8
F	G	A	B♭	C	D	E	F
F		A		C			

ILLUSTRATION 4 b

WRITTEN SCALE

F G A B♭ C D E F

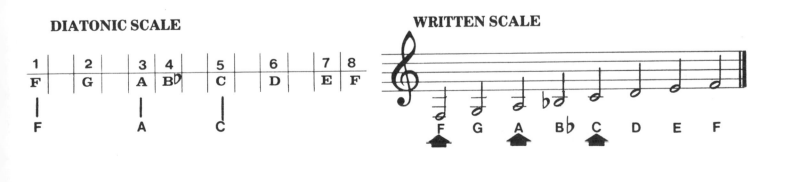

THE "GRAND BARRE" A MOVABLE CHORD

Barre chords allow you to quadruple your chord knowledge. This can be accomplished as each Barre chord can be moved twelve frets, becoming a new chord at each fret.

The Grand Barre chord played at the first fret is an *F* chord. The root note is always on the 6th string for this particular Barre chord. Illustration Four shows the 6th string Chromatic Scale, 12 notes, the complete Chromatic Scale. Thus we can form 12 chords with this one chord alone.

In Illustration One, we show the *F* chord, *F* being the Root on the 6th string. In Illustration Two this chord form has been moved up to the 2nd fret and becomes an *F#* chord. In Illustration Three the chord has been moved up to the third fret and becomes a *G* chord, the *G* note being the note fretted by the Barre finger on the 6th string.

ENHARMONIC CHANGE

The *F#* chord, second fret, may also be called *G♭* as both names appear at the second fret. Either name is correct. Remember: as you progress up the neck you will need to learn some chords by both Enharmonic names. In some Keys a chord may be called by one name and in another Key, by its Enharmonic name. By either name it still sounds the same.

FORM ONE "ROOT" POSITION

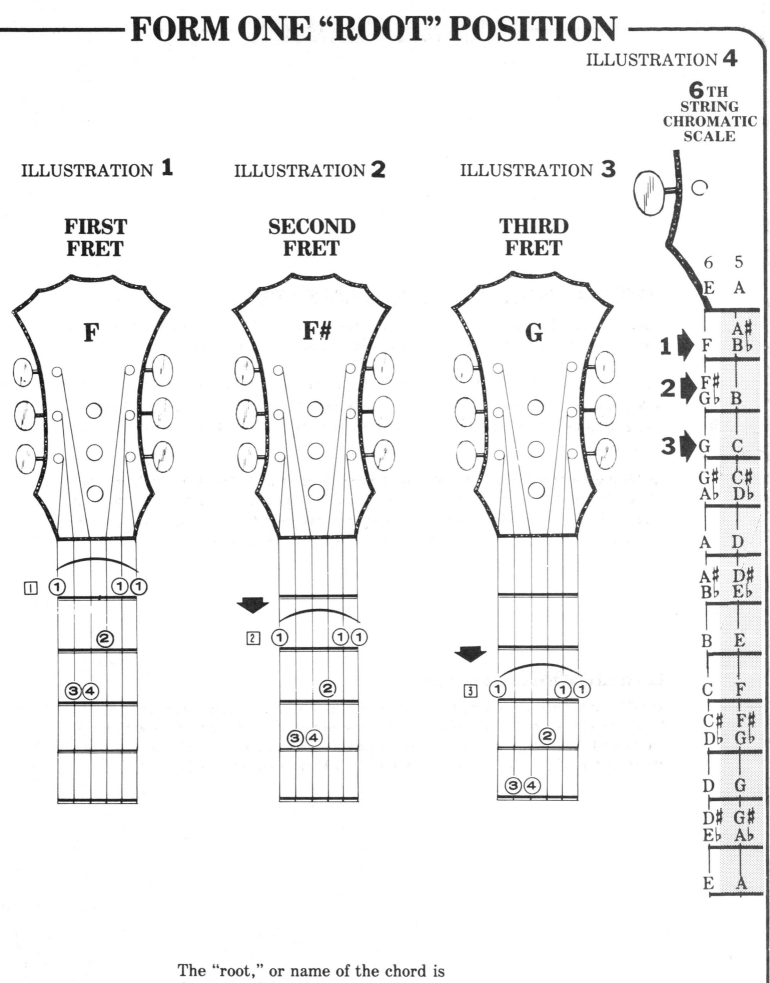

ILLUSTRATION **4**

6TH
STRING
CHROMATIC
SCALE

ILLUSTRATION **1**

ILLUSTRATION **2**

ILLUSTRATION **3**

**FIRST
FRET**

**SECOND
FRET**

**THIRD
FRET**

The "root," or name of the chord is determined by the position of the "Barre" finger on the sixth string.

91

MOVING UP THE NECK

If you have studied "Basic Chord Theory", and "Basic Chords To All Keys", you realize that it is necessary to change finger position for each open string chord. Within the first three frets, the notes of the triad are in different positions for each chord and thus requires a different finger position to play each chord.

With Barre chords this is no longer true. The Triad for the F chord is $F\ A\ C$. At the first fret, the first position, we have this Triad. At every fret a new Triad will appear and the Root note will automatically lock in the rest of the Triad for that particular chord for that fret.

In Illustration Two the Root is A and the notes that automatically appear as the chord is played are only notes of the A chord Triad, $A\ C\#\ E$.

By sliding the chord position up to the 10th fret we have the note D on the sixth string (root note), and the other notes are, again, only notes of the D chord Triad, $D\ F\#\ A$.

This unique sequence of notes appears at each and every fret. No matter at which fret you play this chord form, only those notes that complete the chord Triad named by the Bar finger will appear.

FORM ONE "ROOT" POSITION

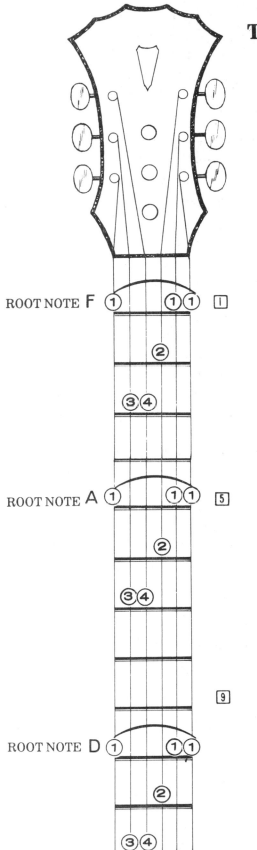

THE BARRE CHORD TRIAD

ROOT NOTE F
1
1 1
2
3 4
1
ROOT NOTE A
1
1 1
2
3 4
5
9
ROOT NOTE D
1
1 1
2
3 4

ILLUSTRATION **1**

FIRST FRET: THE F CHORD

The *F* Chord Triad: *F A C*
Note Sequence: First Fret—
F C F A C F

ILLUSTRATION **2**

FIFTH FRET: THE A CHORD

The *A* Chord Triad: *A C# E*
Note Sequence: Fifth Fret—
A E A C# E A

ILLUSTRATION **3**

TENTH FRET: THE D CHORD

The *D* Chord Triad: *D F# A*
Note Sequence: Tenth Fret—
D A D F# A D

ADDING ADDITIONAL NOTES

The Form one Barre chord, a few alterations, and the Chromatic Scale are the tools that will enable you to play 180 chords. Not only know their names, but also to know that the chord is a 6th, 7th, etc., and you can easily retain this information as you only learn one set of 13 chords and the 6th string chromatic scale.

The *F* chord, Illustration One, is the basic chord position used to accomplish this. As stated previously, this chord position will become a new chord at each fret as it progresses up the neck. It should be noted that if you are using the third and fourth fingers on the 4th and 5th strings to fret this chord you will need to learn an alternate fingering as we must free the fourth finger so it can be used to play additional notes.

The accepted practice is to use the third finger to fret both 4th and 5th strings. In the illustration shown this is shown with the small line drawn over the two notes on the chord diagram, Illustration One B. Should this prove impractical for you, then simply eliminate the 4th string, Illustration One C. However, if it is not fretted, it must be muted, otherwise you will have an unwanted note that will create a dissonant sound.

USING THE LITTLE FINGER

The little finger (4th) is the guitarist's extra hand. Once you can play a full Barre chord without using the little finger, you can immediately put it to use making extra chords for you.

ADDING THE 6th NOTE

The *F6* chord, Illustration Three, is made by using the little finger to add the 6th note of the *F* scale to the *F* chord triad. In our illustration in this section we include the formula for each chord triad, R 3 5, plus the notes that form each chord, *f a c*, etc., and the written chord form as it would appear on sheet music. We also include the horizontal Diatonic Scale, Illustration Five to help you better understand written chords.

By sliding the little finger down on fret from the *F6* position we have the *F7* chord, Illustration Four. The *F7* is more commonly used than the *F6*, however the 6th is used in Jazz and can be a direct substitute for Major type chord.

It will require practice to develop the "stretch" required of the little finger to properly fret the 7th note. However it can be accomplished. Practice playing these chords. It is amazing how pleasant they can sound and you will be able to achieve many different chord progressions without moving the left hand a great deal.

FORM ONE "ROOT" POSITION

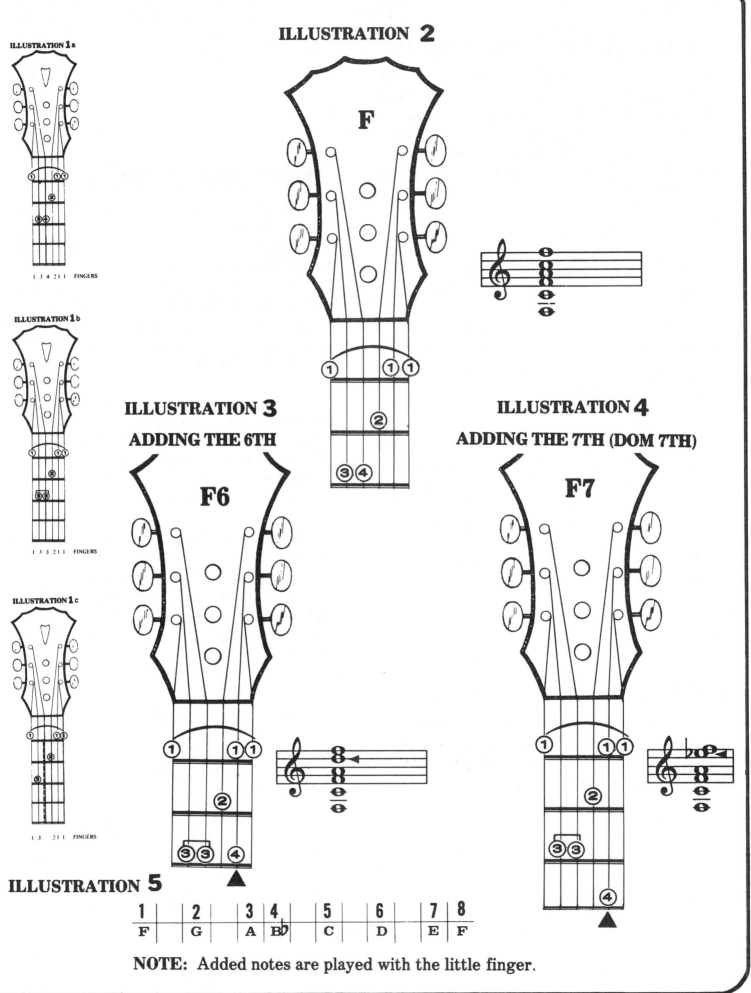

ILLUSTRATION 1a

1 3 4 2 1 1   FINGERS

ILLUSTRATION 1b

1 3 3 2 1 1   FINGERS

ILLUSTRATION 1c

1 3   2 1 1   FINGERS

ILLUSTRATION 2

F

ILLUSTRATION 3
ADDING THE 6TH

F6

ILLUSTRATION 4
ADDING THE 7TH (DOM 7TH)

F7

ILLUSTRATION 5

1	2	3	4		5	6	7	8
F	G	A	B♭		C	D	E	F

NOTE: Added notes are played with the little finger.

FOUR MORE CHORDS

On this page we present four more *F* type chords. The *F Major 7*, *F Diminished*, *F Augmented*, *F Augmented 9*, and the *F Augmented 7*. While these are considered Barre chords, not all are true Barre chords since some do not use all six strings.

However if you consider them as part of the *F* series of Barre chords, you will be able to quickly locate these chords at each fret as they move up the neck.

F MAJ 7

The *F* Major 7th chord is made by adding the 7th note of the *F* scale to the *F* chord triad. This is a "Major 7th" chord and not a "Dominant 7" chord which is constructed with the lowered 7th note. In forming the Major 7 chord we need to move the Root note back one fret, Illustration One. This is a four note chord and is movable. That is, it will become a new chord at each fret. Think of it as an *F* chord with the first note moved back one fret.

In Illustration Two, we show this chord position moved up one fret to the *F#* position. We have done this to show you the full four note fingering which is required to move this chord form up the neck.

F DIM

The *F* Diminshed chord is an *F* chord with the 3rd and 5th notes of the triad lowered one fret, and the 6th note ($\flat\flat$ 7) of the scale added to it. This is only one form of the Diminished chord It is included here as it can be easily identified with the *F* group of chords. The Barre finger is still fretting the *F* note on the 6th string.

F AUG

The *F* augmented chord form shown here is easy to remember as, again, the Root note is on the *F* note on the sixth string. Both the first and sixth string can be considered the Root string as both are *E* Chromatic scales.

SUMMARY

These chords conclude the thirteen Barre chords that can be played at each fret with this chord form. They are all *F* type chords because the Root note is on the 6th string and this note at the first fret is the *F* note. Memorize the 6th string chromatic scale and practice playing these thirteen chords at different frets. It might be noted that as you move up the neck it becomes easier to play them, and it is good practice to do so. **REMEMBER:** Learn the notes on the 6th string, and you will be able to name these chords anywhere on the neck.

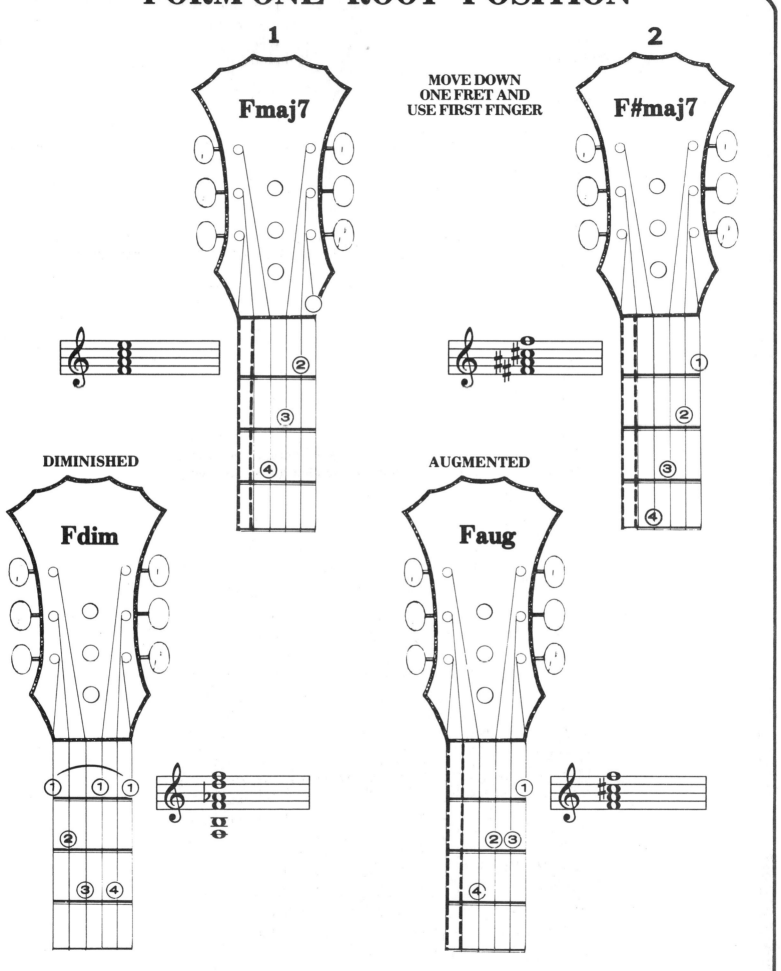

1

Fmaj7

MOVE DOWN
ONE FRET AND
USE FIRST FINGER

2

F#maj7

DIMINISHED

Fdim

AUGMENTED

Faug

The *F* Major chord is made by playing the notes *F A C*. The Root note may be either the lowest note of the chord, on the 6th string, or on the 1st string.

The *F6* chord is an *F* Major chord, *F A C*, plus the additional 6th note of the *F* scale. We add this note to the *F* chord by using the little finger.

THE F 7th

The *F7* chord is made by adding the lowered 7th note of the *F* scale to the *F* chord Triad, Illustration Three. The lowered (flatted) seventh note (E♭) makes this a Dominant 7 chord. Illustration Five shows another form that is commonly used. Study the written chord form and observe the location of the *E♭* note in each chord. Both positions are correct. The 7th position shown in Illustration Three has a more pronounced "leading tone" as the 7th note is on a higher string.

THE F 9th

The *F7add9* chord is made by adding the 9th note of the *F* scale to the *F* chord Triad. Again this added note, as all the others on this page, are made with the little finger. This will require practice if you are not used to stretching four frets from the Barre position.
little finger.

THE F 7th AUG 9

The *F7aug9* is made by adding a "Raised" (Augmented) note of the *F* scale to the *F* chord triad. Again this added note, as all of the others on this page, are made with the little finger. This chord is actually *a Dominant Seventh* chord, and the little finger must fret both the *E♭*, second string, and the *G#*, first string. You must fret both notes with the forth, little, finger.

SUMMARY

So far we have five Barre chords, all made by adding additional notes, as required, with the little finger. You have not moved the Barre finger and since the Root note has not changed, these are all *F* type chords. By moving this position up the neck playing them at each fret through the 12th fret we will have 60 chords.

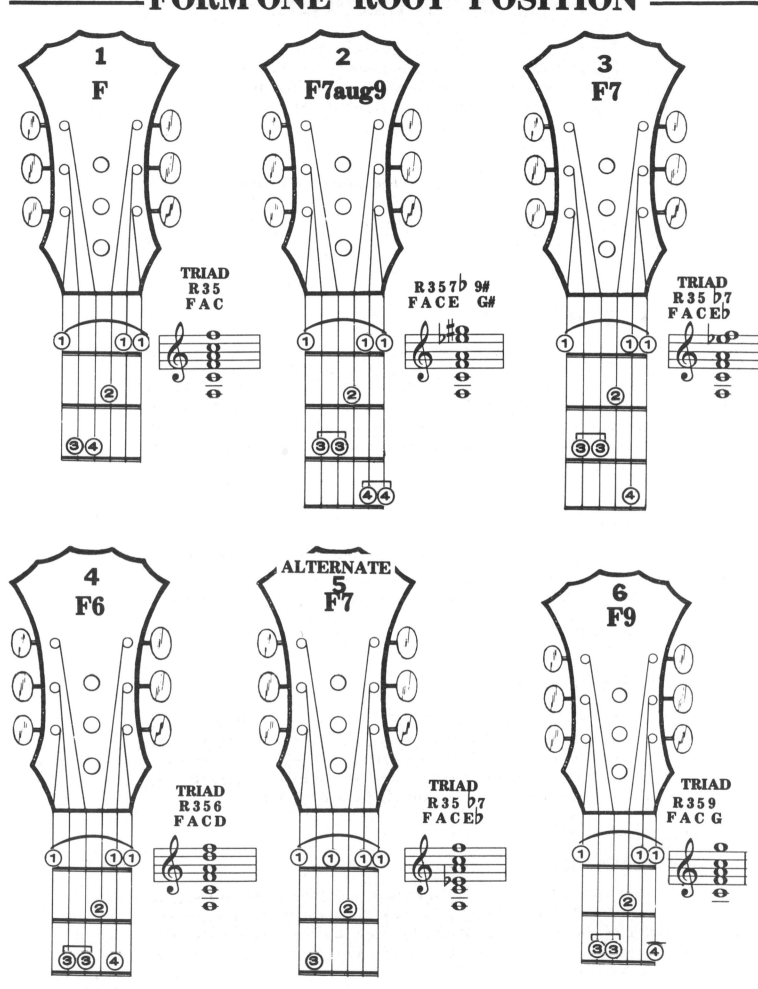

1
F

TRIAD
R 3 5
F A C

2
F7aug9

R 3 5 7♭ 9#
F A C E   G#

3
F7

TRIAD
R 3 5 ♭7
F A C E♭

4
F6

TRIAD
R 3 5 6
F A C D

ALTERNATE
5
F7

TRIAD
R 3 5 ♭7
F A C E♭

6
F9

TRIAD
R 3 5 9
F A C G

THE MINOR POSITION

The *F* Minor chord will appear very similar to the *F* Major chord shown on the previous page. The only difference will be the lowered 3rd required to change *F* Major to *F* Minor. It should be noted that the alterations required to form the minor 6th, 7th, and 9th chords are still made the same way as the Major chord.

F MINOR

To play the *F* Minor chord, form the *F* Major chord and raise the second finger from the third string. You will then have changed *F* Major to *F* Minor lowering the note one half tone, playing a flatted 3rd.

F MINOR 6

The *F* Minor 6 is made by adding the sixth note of the *F* scale to the *F* Minor chord.

F MINOR 7

The *F* Minor 7 is formed by adding the lowered 7th note of the *F* scale to the *F* Minor chord. We show two fingerings for this chord and both are correct. The difference is the placement of the flatted 7th note. One is in the Bass side of the chord, the other is in the upper particial of the chord (treble strings).

F MINOR 9

The *F* Minor add 9th is formed by adding the 9th note of the *F* scale to the *F* Minor chord.

We now know four Minor chords, all played without moving the Barre finger. By sliding these chords up the neck 12 frets you will be able to play 48 Minor chords. These plus the 60 Major chords give you a total of 108 different Barre chords.

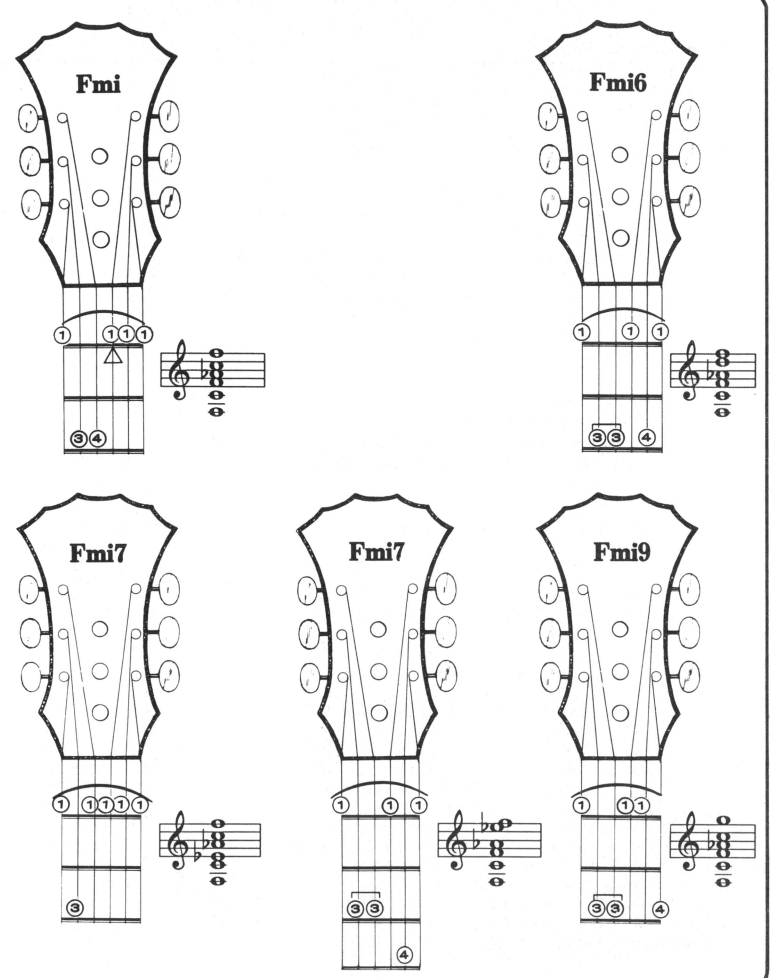

THIRD FRET G TYPE CHORDS

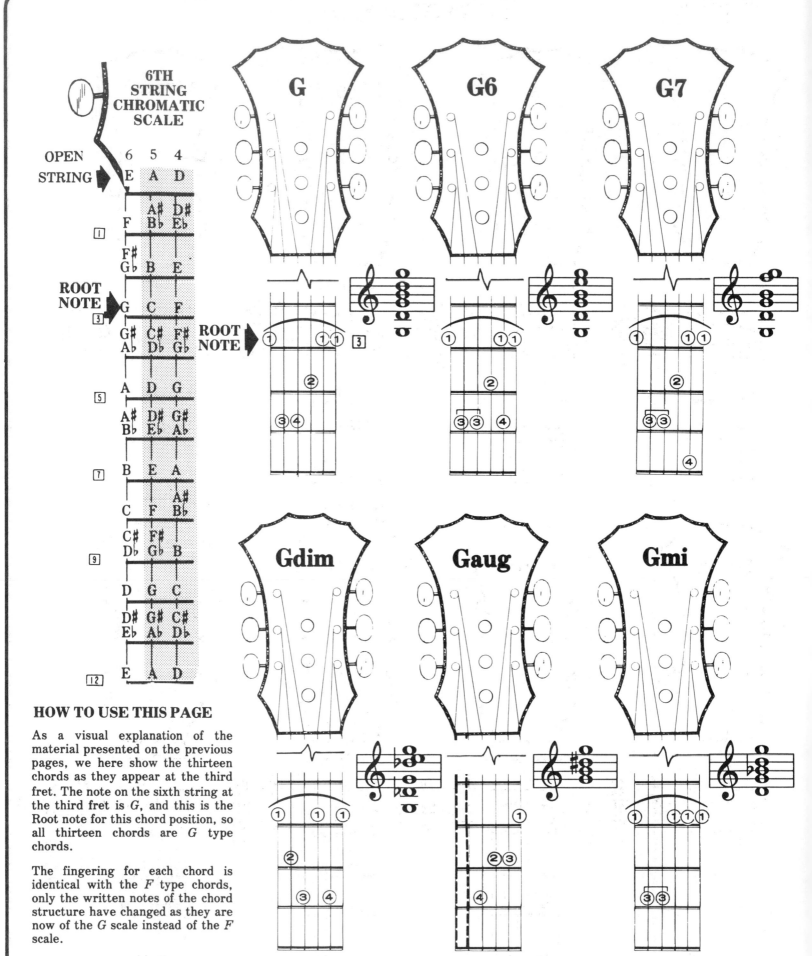

6TH STRING CHROMATIC SCALE

G   G6   G7

Gdim   Gaug   Gmi

HOW TO USE THIS PAGE

As a visual explanation of the material presented on the previous pages, we here show the thirteen chords as they appear at the third fret. The note on the sixth string at the third fret is *G*, and this is the Root note for this chord position, so all thirteen chords are *G* type chords.

The fingering for each chord is identical with the *F* type chords, only the written notes of the chord structure have changed as they are now of the *G* scale instead of the *F* scale.

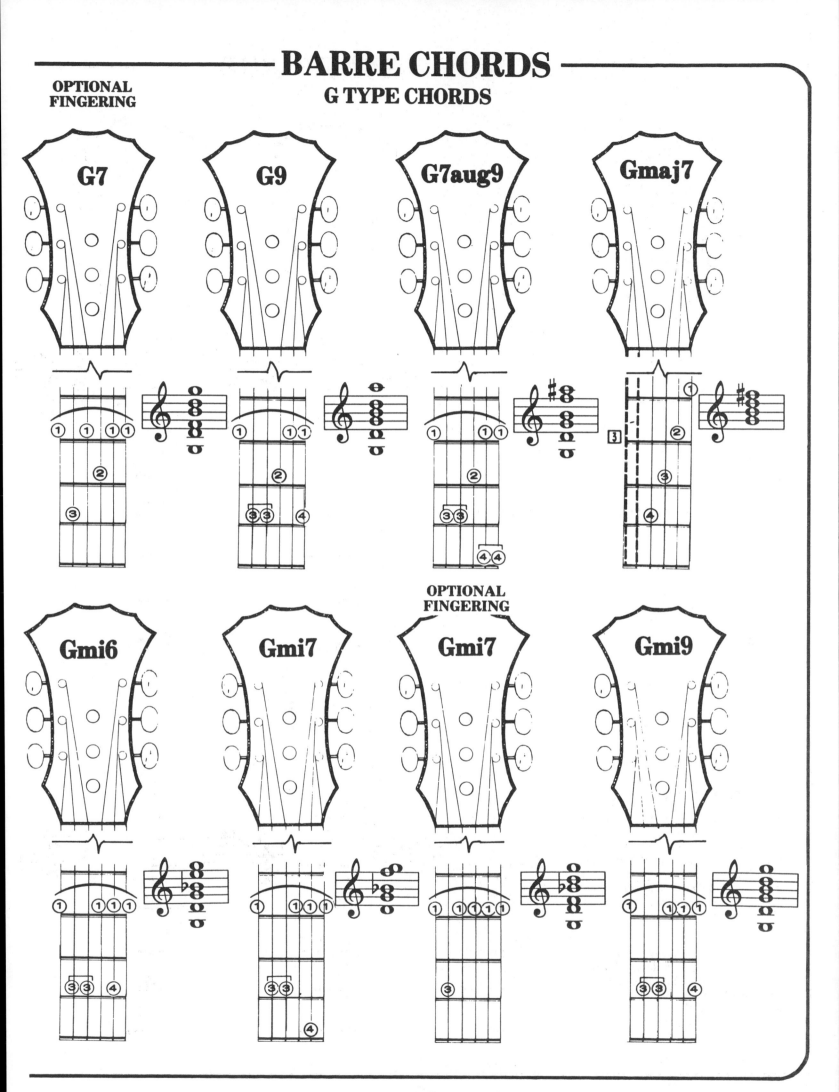

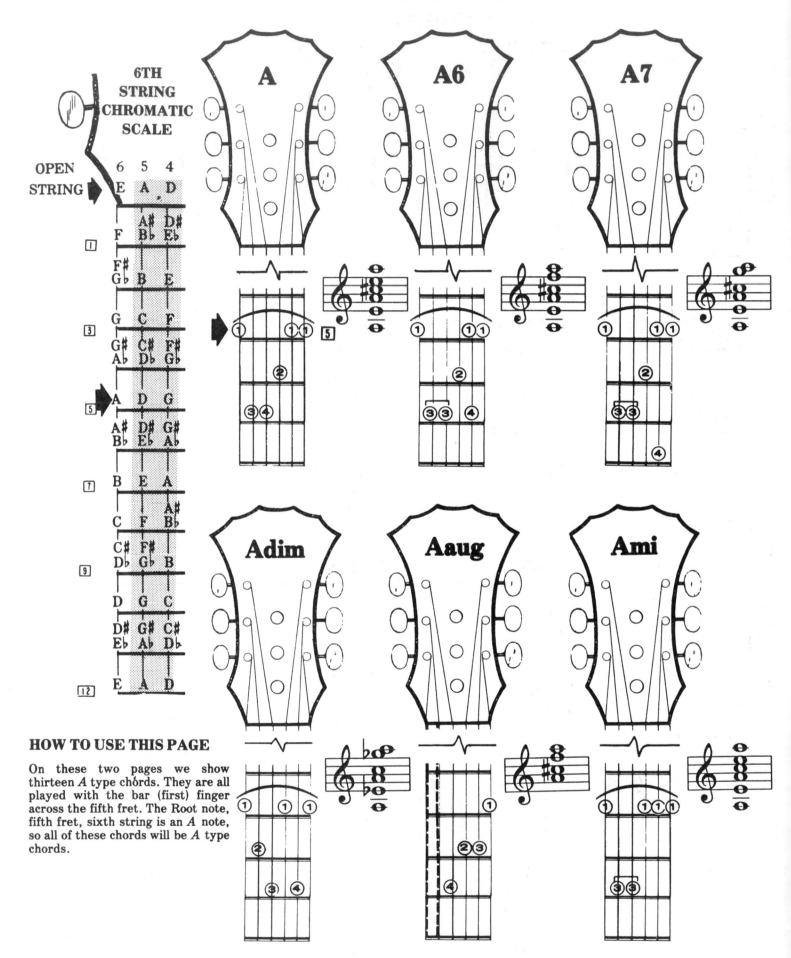

HOW TO USE THIS PAGE

On these two pages we show thirteen *A* type chords. They are all played with the bar (first) finger across the fifth fret. The Root note, fifth fret, sixth string is an *A* note, so all of these chords will be *A* type chords.

BARRE CHORDS
A TYPE CHORDS

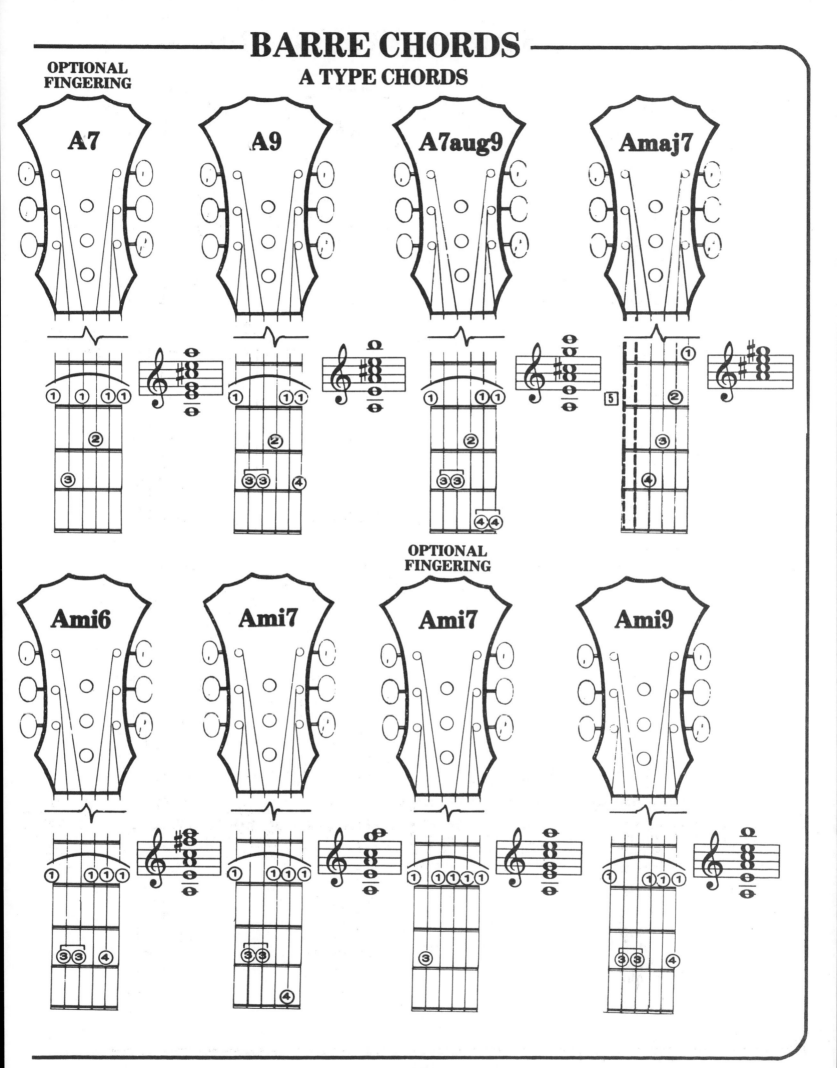

THE C CHORD

The form two Barre chord can be played as a full six string chord, however the five string version is more commonly used.

This is called the FIRST INVERSION. When you can successfully play this form of the Barre chord, you will have the knowledge and ability to play every chord in at least two places on the guitar neck.

To begin, place your fingers in position to play the C chord, Illustration One. **NOTE:** In this position we are not using the sixth string.

ALTERNATE FINGERING

In order to free the first finger for the Barre, change your fingering to the position shown in Illustration Two, keeping the first finger free.

A MOVABLE CHORD

Now slide your hand up a few frets and lay the First finger across the first three strings barring them. This now is a "movable" chord and can be played at every fret.

ILLUSTRATION 1

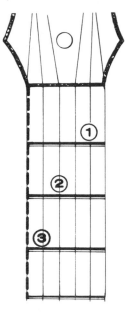

THE C CHORD

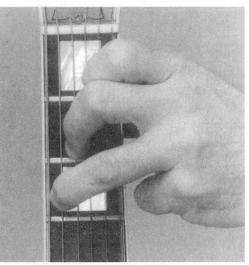

NOW — SUBSTITUTE ALTERNATE FINGERING

ILLUSTRATION 2

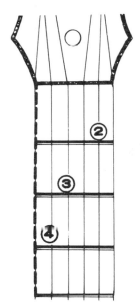

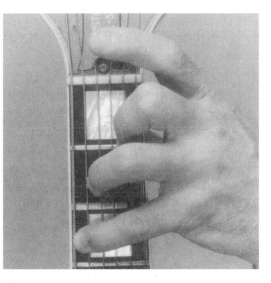

THE MOVABLE CHORD

ILLUSTRATION 3

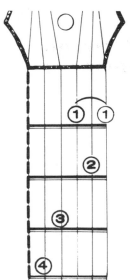

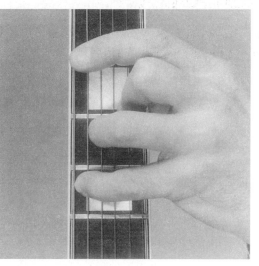

BARRE CHORDS

ALTERNATE FINGERING

The form two first inversion chord can be played several ways. Study these different forms, and learn to play all of them. In rhythm work you will find advantages in knowing all three.

FIRST ALTERNATE FINGERING

This is the full six string form of this chord, Illustration One. The first, or bar finger reaches over and frets the sixth string. The note produced on the sixth string usually does not sound well with the chord even though the tone produced is a note of the chord triad. This is due to the low octave sound beating against the higher tones of the closely related higher sounding tones.

SECOND ALTERNATE FINGERING

This is the most commonly used form of the chord, Illustration Two. The sixth string is muted. The first finger bars only three strings and this eliminates strain on the wrist and is usually easier to change to other chords.

THIRD ALTERNATE FINGERING

This form, Illustration Three, allows us to play a full six string chord, however it is difficult to fret both bass strings with the fourth finger. In some rhythm work, you can alternate the fourth finger between these two strings when playing a "pick and strum" type of rhythm.

THE DIATONIC SCALE—KEY OF D

The diatonic scale for the Key of D shows the three notes that form the D chord. The Major triad being built on the 1st, 3rd and 5th notes of the scale—D F# A.

FORM TWO
ALTERNATE FINGERING

ILLUSTRATION 1

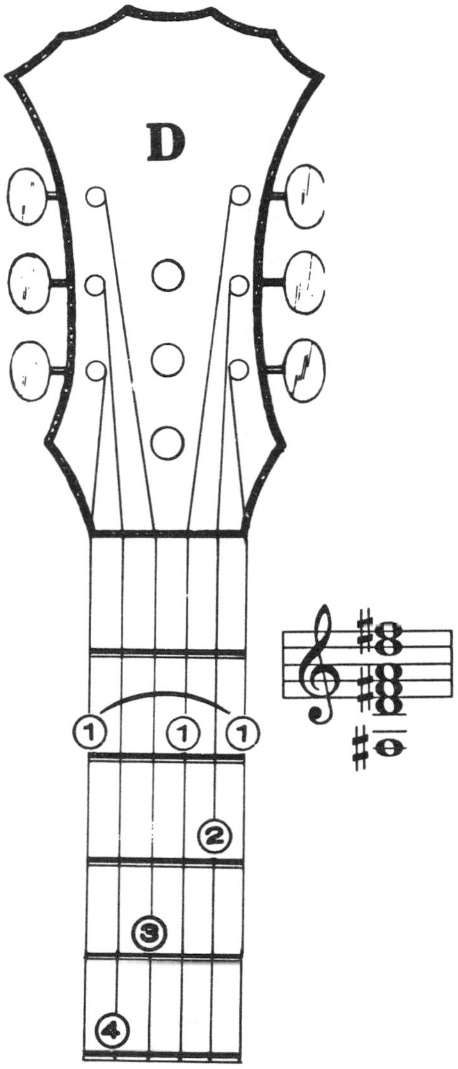

D

FULL 6 STRING CHORD

ILLUSTRATION 2

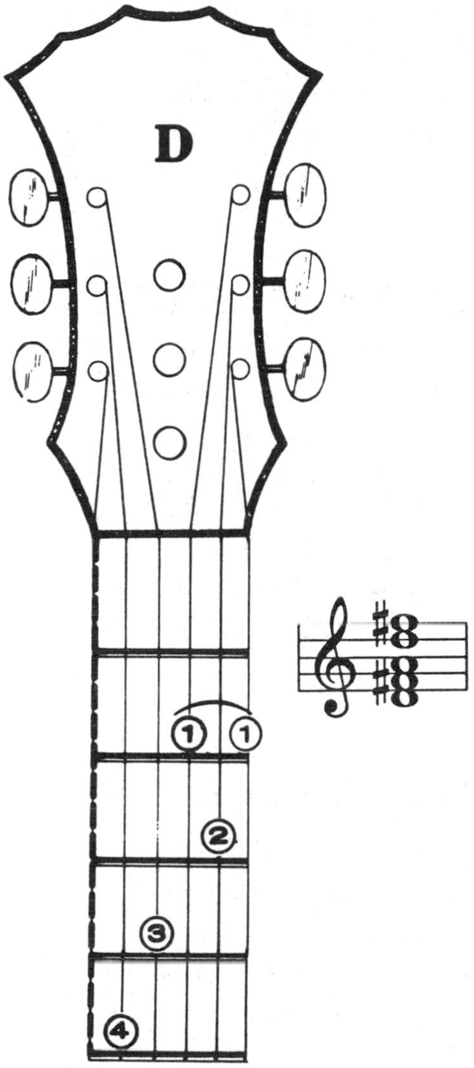

D

**SHORT BARRE
5 STRING CHORD**

ILLUSTRATION 3

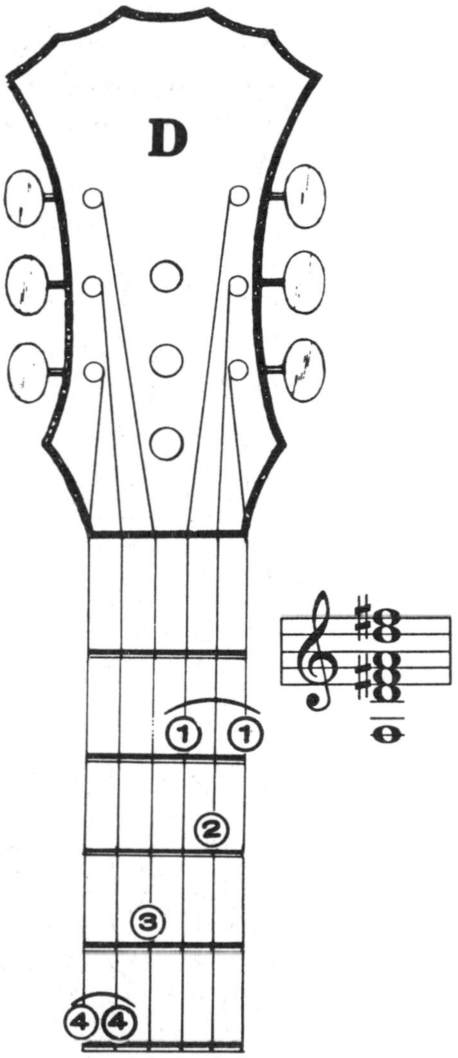

D

**SHORT BARRE
6 STRING CHORD**

KEY OF D

DIATONIC SCALE

1	2	3	4	5	6	7	8
D	E	F#	G	A	B	C#	D
D		F#		A		= D CHORD TRIAD	

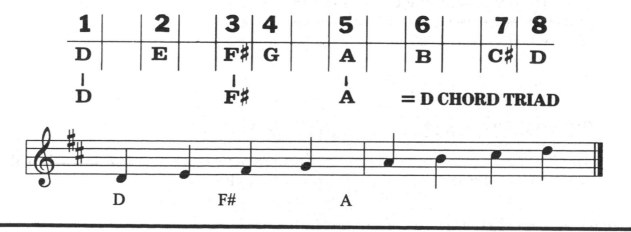

D   F#   A

C# CHORD

In playing the form two barre chord the Root note appears twice, once on the fifth string and again on the second string.

The student should be familiary with the Chromatic on both strings and practice playing the chords on different frets. For our purpose we will use the second string for establishing the Root note. We do this since many times we use the short form eliminating the fourth string.

The C# chord is the first position of the Form Two Barre chord that can be barred with the first finger, Illustration One. Moved back one fret the "Nut" becomes the Barre and we have the C chord. Once the chord is moved up to the C# position and the first finger Barre is made, the chord becomes completely movable.

The notes fretted by the second finger, second string determines the chord name. This Root note moves up and down the second string chromatic scale, Illustration Five.

A MOVABLE CHORD

By placing the first finger across the second fret we have the *D* chord, Illustration Two. The second finger, second string will be fretting the *D* note. You are possibly more familiar with the three finger, open string, chord which is a simpler version of this Barre chord. By barring, we have the *D* chord in a movable position.

Sliding the Barre up to the third fret, Illustration Three, we have the *D#* chord. Slide up one more fret and we are playing the *E* chord, Illustration Four. Notice how the Root note progresses up the second string chromatic scale naming the chord at each fret.

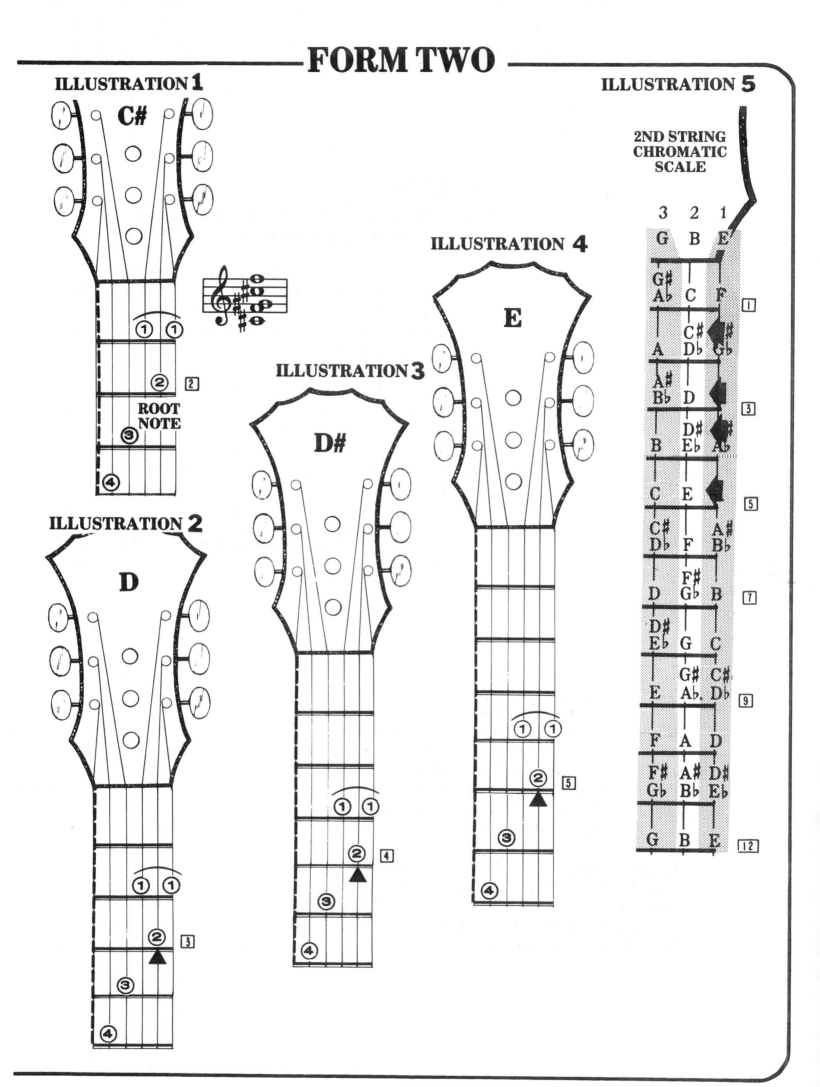

MOVING UP THE NECK

If you have studied *Basic Chord Theory* and *Basic Chords to All Keys*, you are familiar with chord triads. A Major chord is built on the first, third, and fifth notes of a Diatonic Scale, and only these notes may be used. Adding any other note, or notes, changes the chord either to a pleasant sounding altered chord, or to an unpleasant dissonant chord.

The advantage of Barre chords is the fact that at each fret you produce a true chord. At the second fret, only the notes *D F# A* are fretted, and these are the notes of the *D* chord.

If the chord position is moved up to the seventh fret, only the notes *G B D* are fretted and these are the notes that form the *G* chord.

ROOT NOTE

For our study of chords we use the second string for placement of the Root note.

In actual chord theory this would be in the treble octave of the scale, while the Root note on the fifth string is in the bass octave, sounding one octave lower.

FORM TWO
MOVING UP THE NECK

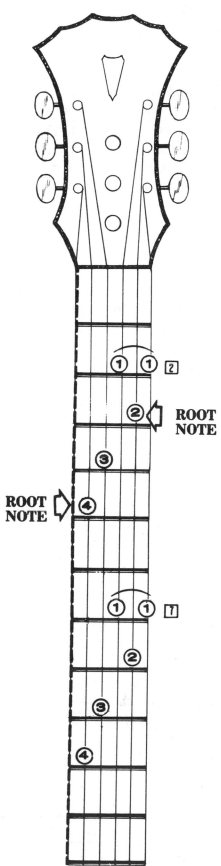

SECOND FRET: THE D CHORD

**D CHORD TRIAD: D F# A
NOTE SEQUENCE, SECOND FRET
F# D A D F#**

SEVENTH FRET: THE G CHORD

**G CHORD TRIAD: G B D
NOTE SEQUENCE, SEVENTH FRET
B G B D G B**

ADDING NOTES

There are many variations to each Major chord and these are called "altered chords". The Major chord is constructed by playing simultaneously the first, third and fifth notes of a scale. This is the basic chord triad. To alter a Major chord we can sharpen a note of the Triad, flatten a note or the Triad, or add additional notes to the Triad. Thus we can have a *D, Dmi, D6, D7, DMaj7*, etc. In each example the basic Triad has been altered or notes added to make the change. Illustrations Five, the horizontal Diatonic scale, will enable the student to better understand chord construction.

THE D6 CHORD

Illustration One, shows the *D* chord. the *D* chord Triad is *D F# A*. We are not using the sixth string for reasons explained on the previous pages. The *D6* chord, Illustration Two, is based on the *D* chord Triad with the added 6th note of the scale, the note *B* also played as part of the chord. To fret the *D6*, we move the third finger back to the fourth string and use the little finger to play the 6th note on the third string.

THE D7 CHORD

The *D7* chord is a Dominant 7th Type chord as we are adding the lowered 7th note of the *D* scale, the note *C*. Notice the correct fingering. Here the little finger moves up one fret, from the *B* note (6th) to the *C* note, the lowered 7th note.

THE D MAJOR 7 CHORD

The *D Major 7* chord is, again, a *D* chord with the 7th note, not lowered, added to the chord. Illustration Four shows the accepted fingering.

ILLUSTRATION 5

THE DIATONIC SCALE—KEY OF D

1	2	3	4	5	6	7	8
D	E	F#	G	A	B	C#	D

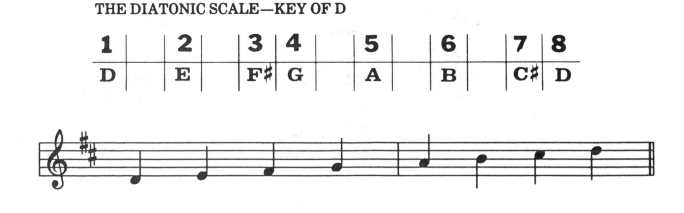

FORM TWO

ILLUSTRATION **1**

D

R 3 5
D F# A

ILLUSTRATION **2**

D6

R 3 5 6
D F# A B

ILLUSTRATION **3**

D7

R 3 5 ♭7
D F# A C

ILLUSTRATION **4**

Dmaj7

R 3 5 7
D F# A C#

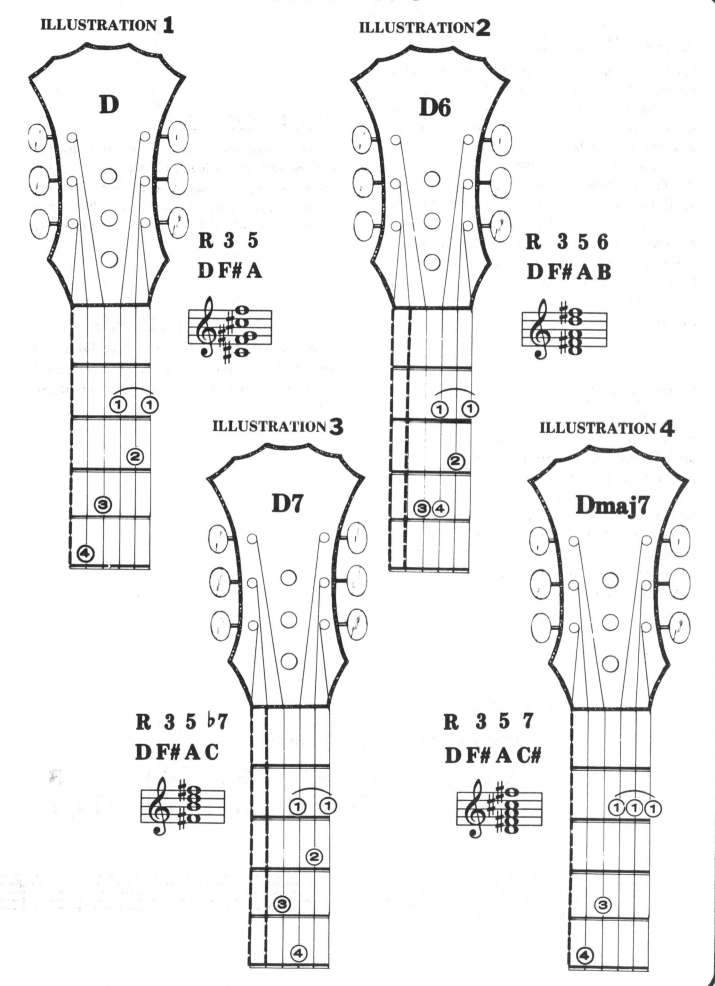

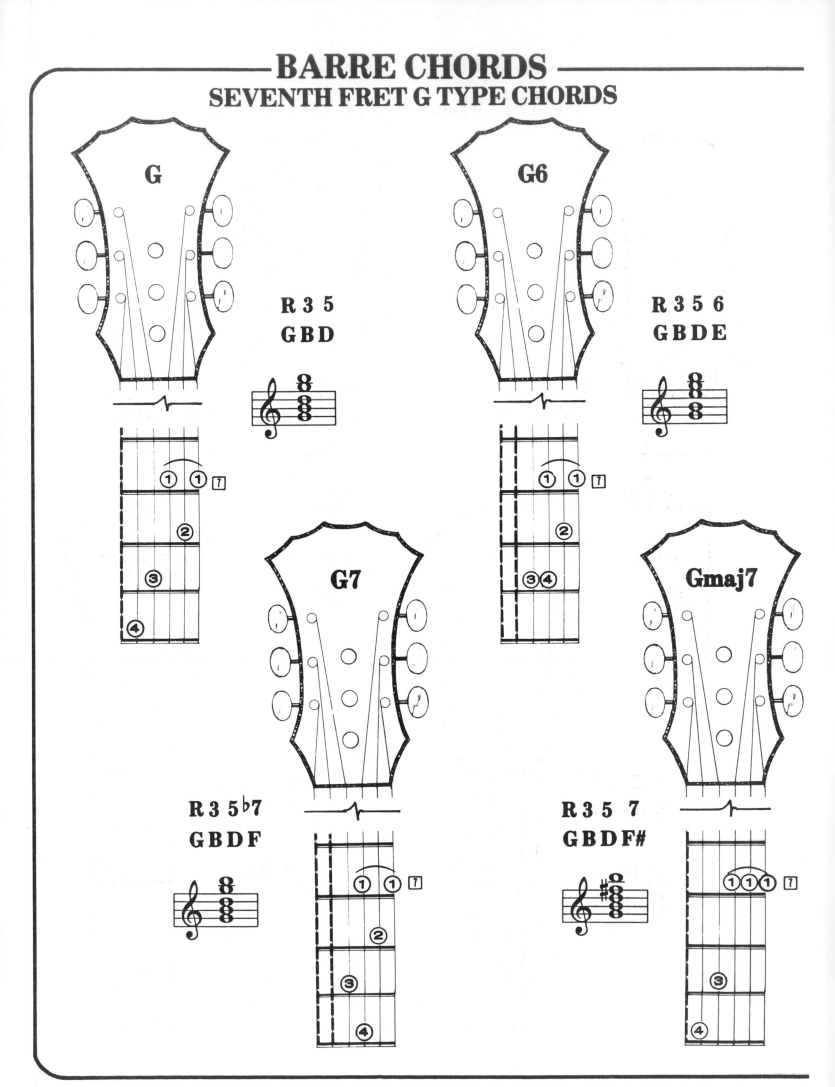

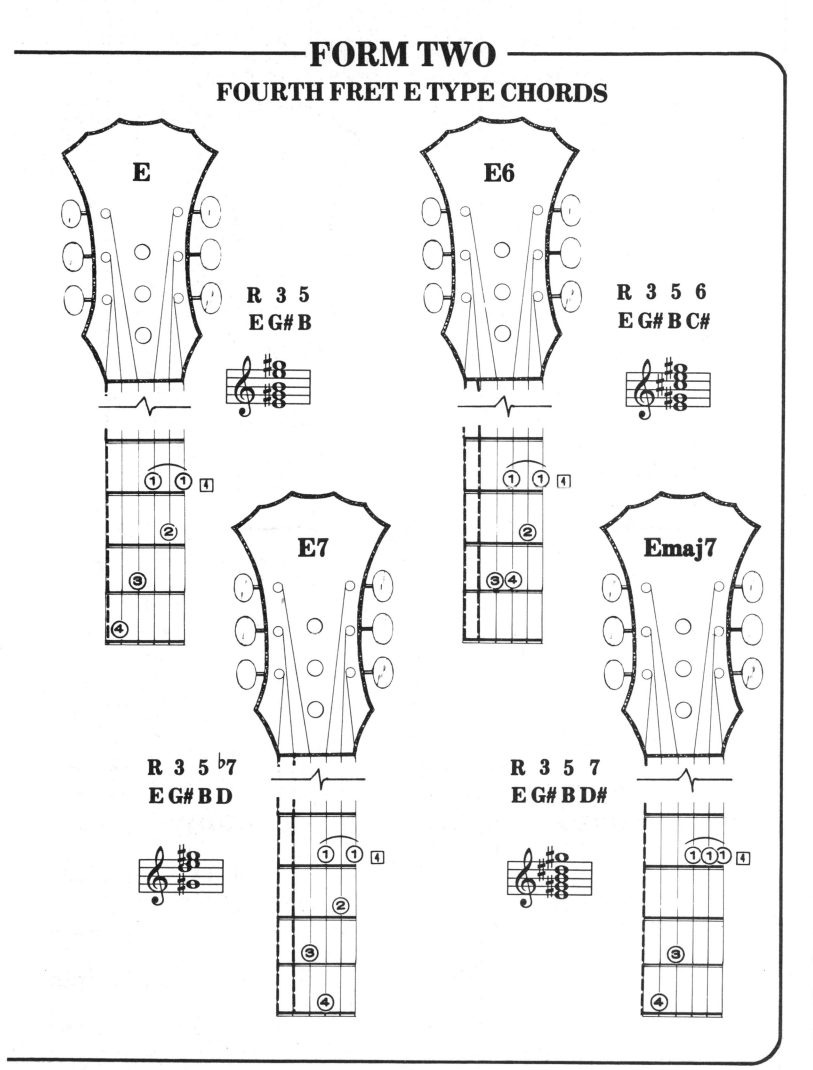

E

R 3 5
E G# B

E6

R 3 5 6
E G# B C#

E7

R 3 5 ♭7
E G# B D

Emaj7

R 3 5 7
E G# B D#

FORM THREE

Before we begin let us take a closer look at this form of the Barre chord. Illustration One shows the chord as it will normally appear in chord arrangements. The Root note is on the third string so we use the third string Chromatic scale to determine the name of the chord at each fret.

Since we show the chord being played at the first fret, it is a $B\flat$ chord. The written chord, Illustration Two, will show the notes stacked as they appear when the chord is actually played.

Illustration Three shows one method of placing the fingers in position to play this chord. Illustration Four shows the horizontal Diatonic Scale for the Key of $B\flat$. The Triad is formed by using the first, third and fifth notes of the Scale, the notes $B\flat$ D and E.

FORM THREE

ILLUSTRATION 1

B♭

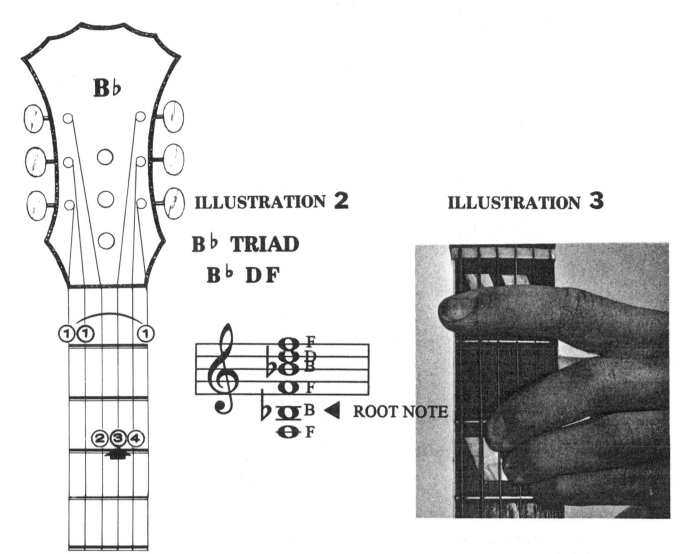

ILLUSTRATION 2

B♭ TRIAD

B♭ D F

F
D
B
F
B ◄ ROOT NOTE
F

ILLUSTRATION 3

ILLUSTRATION 4

KEY OF B♭ TWO FLATS B♭ E♭

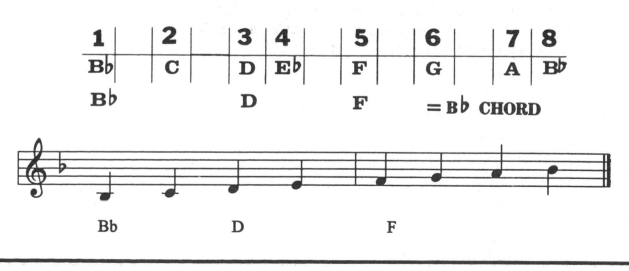

1	2	3	4	5	6	7	8
B♭	C	D	E♭	F	G	A	B♭
B♭		D		F	= B♭ CHORD		

Bb   D   F

THE A CHORD

To begin, place your fingers in position to play the standard three finger *A* chord, Illustration One.

ALTERNATE FINGERING

We must free the first finger in order to use it as the Bar, so substitute the alternate fingering as shown in Illustration Two, keeping the first finger free.

THE MOVABLE BARRE CHORD

Now slide your hand down a few frets keeping your fingers in position. Then place your first finger across the neck, fretting the fifth string with the end of the first finger at the same time fretting the first string with the upper part of the Bar finger.

FORM THREE

ILLUSTRATION 1

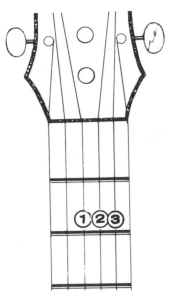

BASE POSITION, THE A CHORD

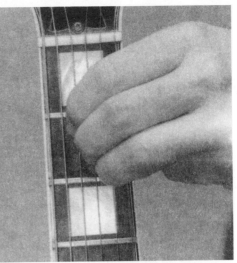

NOW—SUBSTITUTE ALTERNATE FINGERING

ILLUSTRATION 2

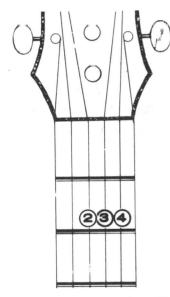

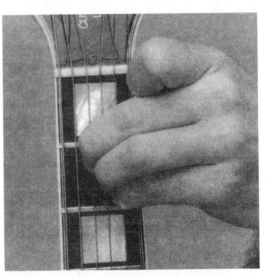

THE MOVABLE "BARRE" CHORD

ILLUSTRATION 3

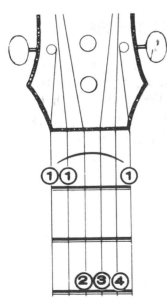

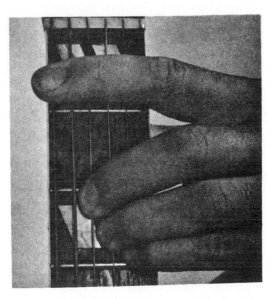

THREE FINGER POSITION

There are three acceptable finger formations that are
commonly used in playing the form Three Barre chord.
The finger position shown on the previous page is used
by most students. However it limits our playing as we
have tied down the fourth finger which is needed when
playing added notes. Illustration One shows one way of
playing the chord by using the second finger, represented by the line over the two notes, to fret two strings.

TWO FINGER POSITION

Illustration Two shows another form whereby the third
finger is barred across all three strings. The student
should experiment with all three positions and use the
one best suited to his abilities.

FORM THREE
ALTERNATE FINGERING

ILLUSTRATION 1

ILLUSTRATION 2

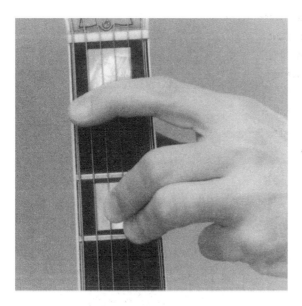

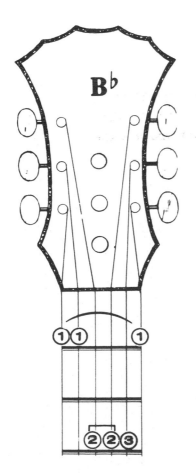

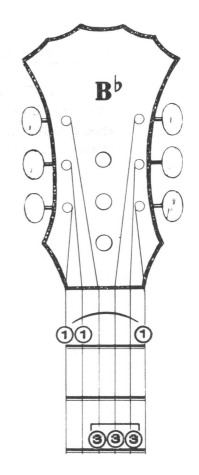

A MOVABLE CHORD

The usage of the Barre makes Barre chords movable. They can be placed at any fret since we are not using any open unfretted strings. The form Three Barre chord becomes a new chord at each fret through the 12th fret, then starts repeating again.

The Root note for this chord is on the *G* or 3rd string. Whatever note is being fretted by the second finger will automatically name the chord. Illustration Four represents the Chromatic Scale on the *G* string. With the Barre finger across the first fret, Illustration One, we have a *B♭* chord. By moving the chord up one fret it becomes a *B* chord. Sliding up one more fret we have the *C* chord, Illustration Three.

THE ROOT OR NAME OF THE FORM THREE CHORD IS DETERMINED BY THE POSITION OF THE "BARRE" FINGER ON THE CHROMATIC SCALE OF THE 3RD STRING.

FORM THREE
MOVING UP THE NECK

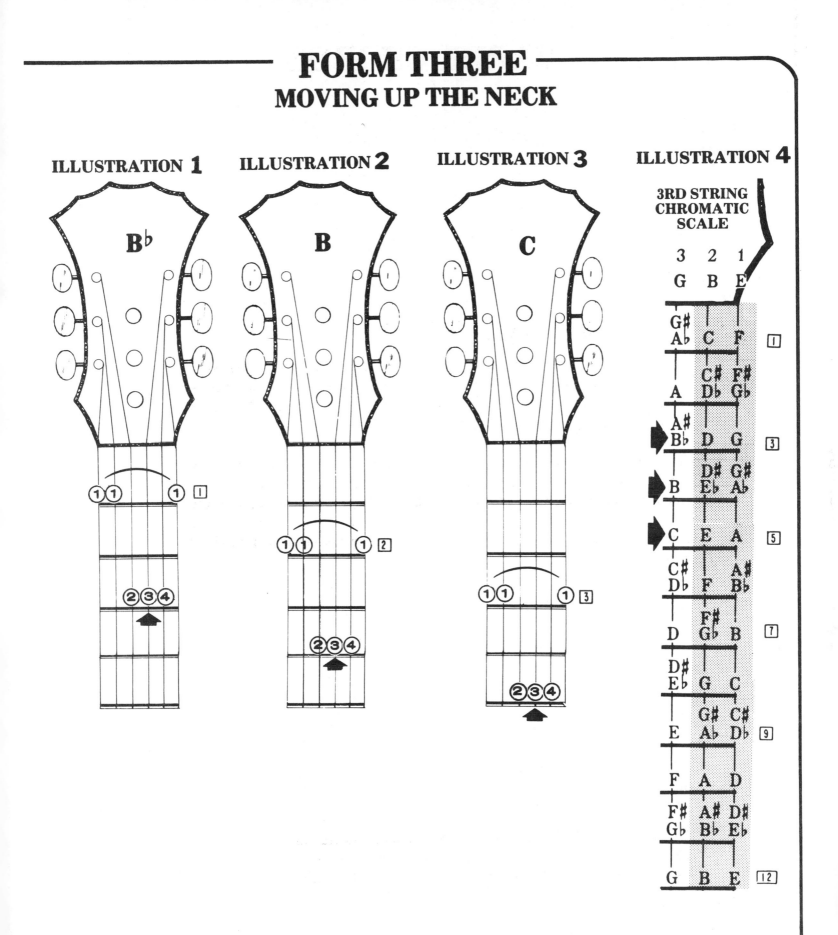

ILLUSTRATION **1**

B♭

ILLUSTRATION **2**

B

ILLUSTRATION **3**

C

ILLUSTRATION **4**

3RD STRING
CHROMATIC
SCALE

MOVING UP THE NECK

When playing this form of the Barre chord at the first fret we have the $B\flat$ chord. The Root note will be on the third string. All of the notes produced in playing this chord will be only notes of the $B\flat$ chord Triad—$B\flat$ D F. The Root note locks in all of the other notes to form this chord.

For example, when the Barre finger is at the fifth fret the root note is on a D note. All other notes formed by the chord are notes of the D chord Triad, D $F\#$ A.

At the twelfth fret the Root note is G and all notes produced by playing the form three chord are G Triad notes—G B D.

PLAYING TIP

The greatest advantage is using the form three Barre chord is the ease with which you can switch from the Tonic chord to the Sub Dom chord in any key without having to move the first finger. EXAMPLE: If you are playing in the Key of A the Tonic chord would be A. If we use the Form One as the Root position at the fifth fret to play the A chord, we can keep the Barre finger in position and simply change to the Form Three chord to play the Sub Dom chord, the D chord. To play the Dominant E chord, simply slide the Form three from the Fifth fret, the D chord, up two frets to play the E chord at the seventh fret.

FORM THREE
MOVING UP THE NECK

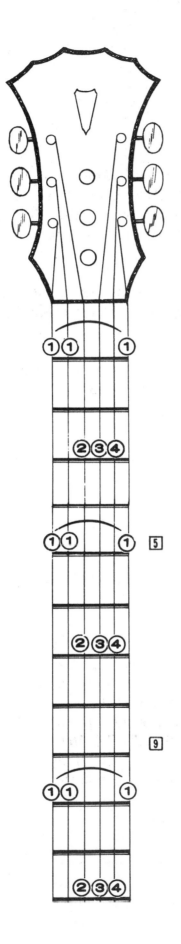

FIRST FRET: THE B♭ CHORD
B♭ CHORD TRIAD B♭ D F
NOTE SEQUENCE FIRST FRET
F B♭ F B♭ D F

FIFTH FRET: THE D CHORD
D CHORD TRIAD D F# A
NOTE SEQUENCE FIFTH FRET

A D A D F# A

TENTH FRET: THE G CHORD
G CHORD TRIAD G B D
NOTE SEQUENCE TENTH FRET
D G D G B E D

ADDING NOTES

With simply one finger changes in the Form Three chord we can easily make six chords. The chords are grouped in this manner to help the student learn them easier. If you were asked to play an $Eb\,mi7$ chord, could you? Actually you would need only to make an Eb chord at the eighth fret, convert it into a mi7 chord and presto—an $Eb\,mi7$ chord.

We use the Bb chord in this explanation as it is the first chord we can play with the Form three chord form. You may want to practice playing this position further up the neck, as it becomes easier to play when moved to a higher position.

THE B♭ 6 CHORD

The Bb 6th chord is constructed by adding the 6th note of the Bb scale to the Bb chord Triad (R 3 5 6). This note is added to the basic Bb chord by placing the little finger on the first string at the third fret, Illustration Two.

THE B♭ 7 (Dom 7)

The Bb 7 chord is made by adding the lowered 7th note of the Bb Scale to the Bb chord triad (R 3 5 b7), Illustration Three. The added note is on the first string at the fourth fret and is fretted with the little finger. This is a Dominant 7th type chord, not a Major 7th, as we are adding a flatted 7th note. Illustration Four shows an alternate position that should be practiced. It will sound different as the 7th note has been added in the lower part of the chord and will not be as pronounced as one played on the higher sounding treble strings.

THE B♭ MINOR CHORD

The Bb Minor chord is formed by lowering the third note of the Bb scale to the Bb chord Triad (R b3 5). This is accomplished by simply moving the D note back one fret. It will be necessary to change the fingering, using the second finger to play the Minor note, Illustration Five.

THE B♭ MINOR 7 CHORD

The Bb Minor 7 chord is built on the Bb Minor Triad (R b3 5 b7). First change the Bb chord to a Bb Minor and then add the lowered 7th note of the Bb scale to the chord, Illustration Six.

FORM THREE

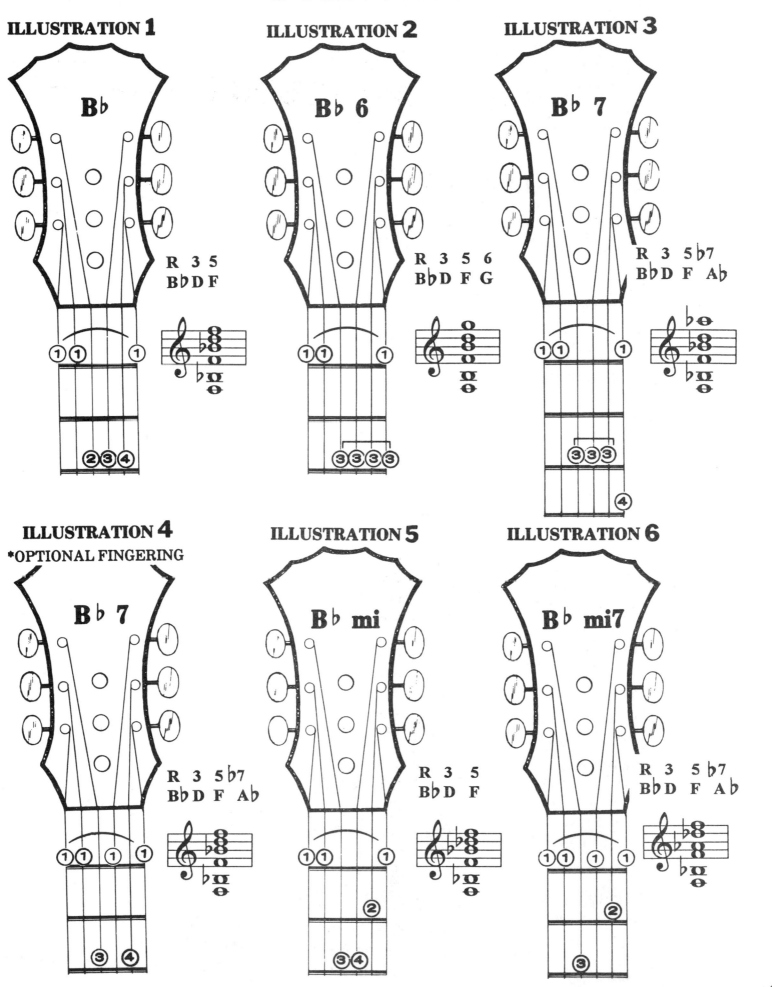

ILLUSTRATION 1

B♭

R 3 5
B♭ D F

ILLUSTRATION 2

B♭ 6

R 3 5 6
B♭ D F G

ILLUSTRATION 3

B♭ 7

R 3 5 ♭7
B♭ D F A♭

ILLUSTRATION 4

*OPTIONAL FINGERING

B♭ 7

R 3 5 ♭7
B♭ D F A♭

ILLUSTRATION 5

B♭ mi

R 3 5
B♭ D F

ILLUSTRATION 6

B♭ mi7

R 3 5 ♭7
B♭ D F A♭

THE MAJOR 7 CHORD

We can further alter the $B\flat$ chord by making it into a Major Seventh chord, Illustration One. The Major 7 chord is built by adding the 7th note of the scale to the $B\flat$ chord Triad (R 3 5 7). It is important to remember that the Dominant 7th chord is built with the LOWERED 7th note, whereas the Major 7 chord is built with the SEVENTH note (unaltered). When playing chords such as $g7$, $c7$, $b\flat7$, etc., you are playing Dominant 7th type chords. All Major 7th chords are written as: *G Maj 7, C Maj 7*, etc.

The Major 7 chord is popular with Jazz guitarists and is often used as an ending chord in Rock music.

The form shown here is one of two illustrated in this Book. We include this form here because it is a modification of the Form Three chord and should be thought of as an altered Form three chord form.

THE MAJOR SEVENTH

ILLUSTRATION 1

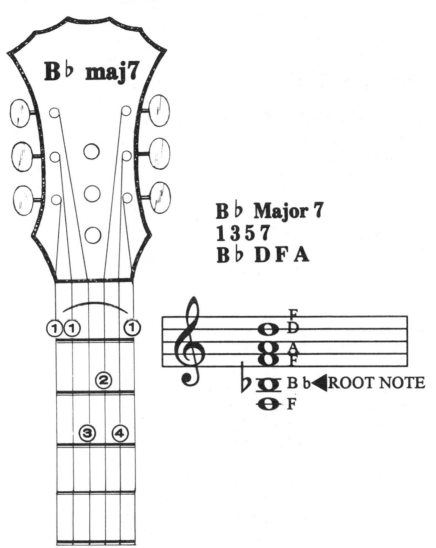

B♭ Major 7
1 3 5 7
B♭ D F A

ILLUSTRATION 2

KEY OF B♭ TWO FLATS B♭ E♭

1	2	3	4	5	6	7	8
B♭	C	D	E♭	F	G	A	B♭

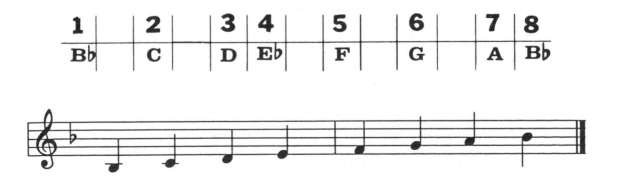

C TYPE CHORDS

Here we have moved the *Bb* chord position up to the third fret. These seven chords are in the *C* position at the third fret. The Root note fretted by the Barre finger is the *C* note on the third string.

PLAYING TIP

The exercise below will aid in understanding the relationship between the Form One Barre chord and the Form Three type chord form.

This is a study in the usage of these two types of Barre chords in playing the Tonic, Sub Dom, and Dom type chords.

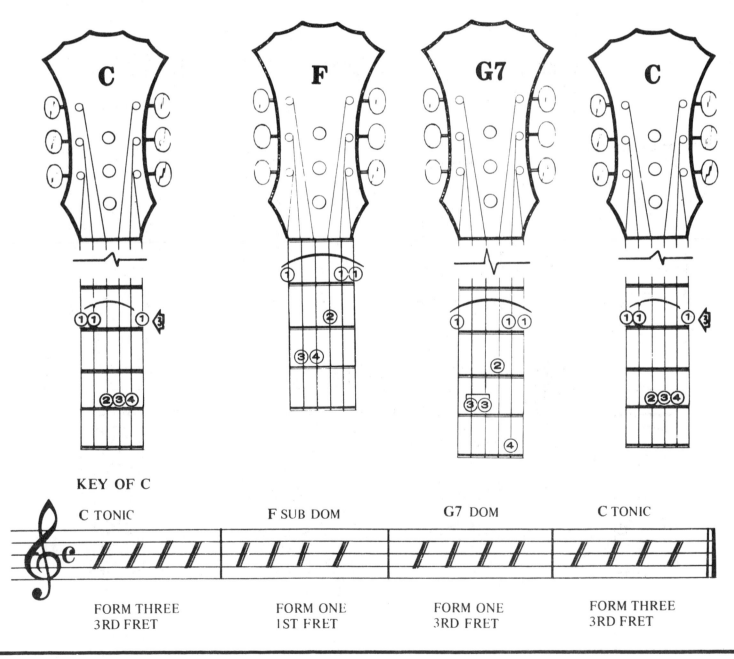

KEY OF C

C TONIC	F SUB DOM	G7 DOM	C TONIC
FORM THREE 3RD FRET	FORM ONE 1ST FRET	FORM ONE 3RD FRET	FORM THREE 3RD FRET

FORM THREE
C TYPE CHORDS

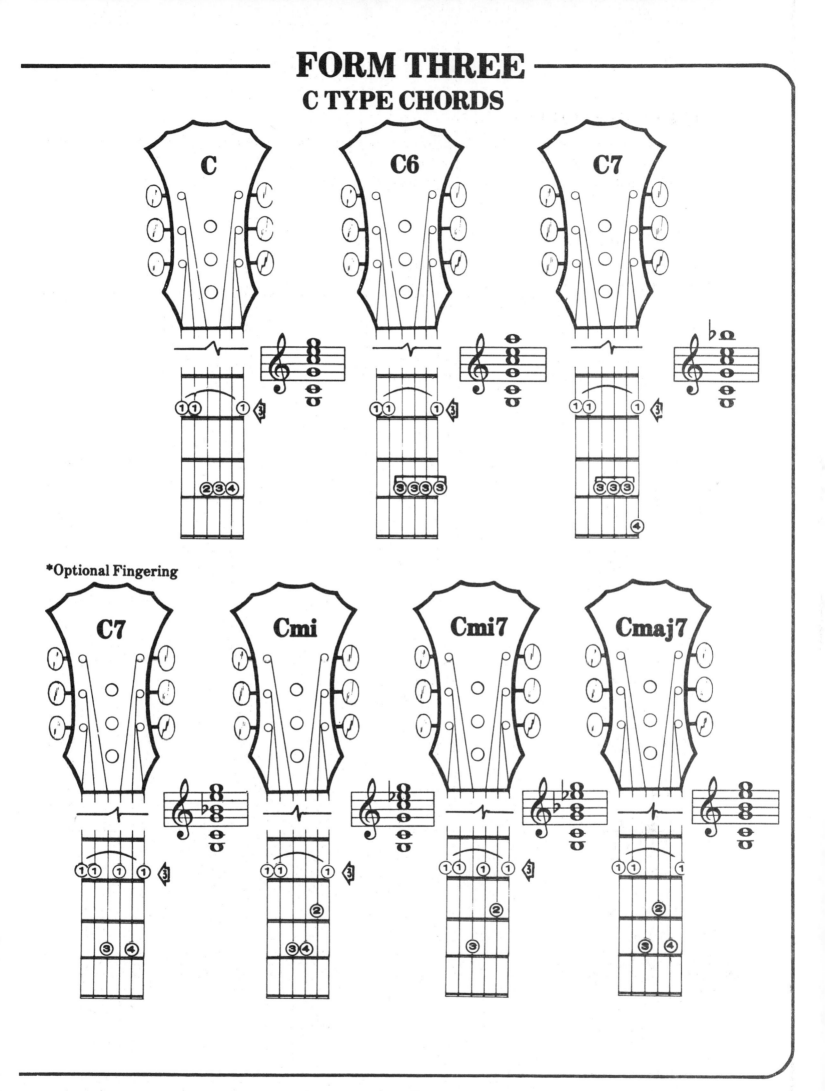

*Optional Fingering

BARRE CHORDS
D TYPE CHORDS

At the fifth fret we have the *D* chord using the Form Three Barre chords. The Root note, third string is the note *D*. These seven chords can be played without moving the Barre finger.

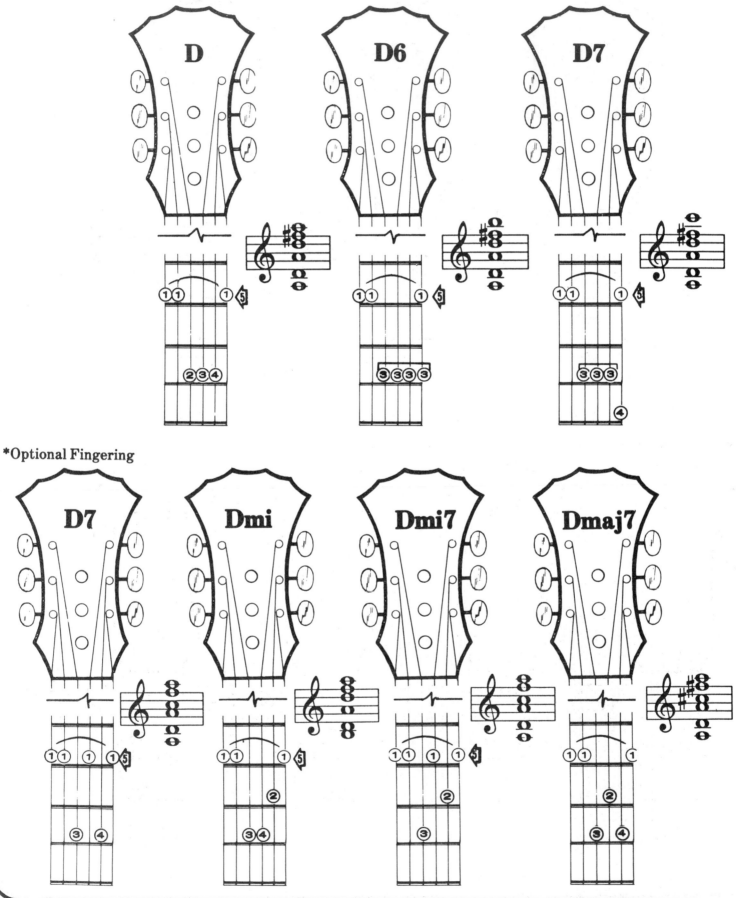

*Optional Fingering

FORM THREE
E TYPE CHORDS

When the Form Three Barre chord is played at the seventh fret we have all *E* type chords. Again the Root note, third string is the note *E*. Try practicing all of these chords without lifting the Barre finger.

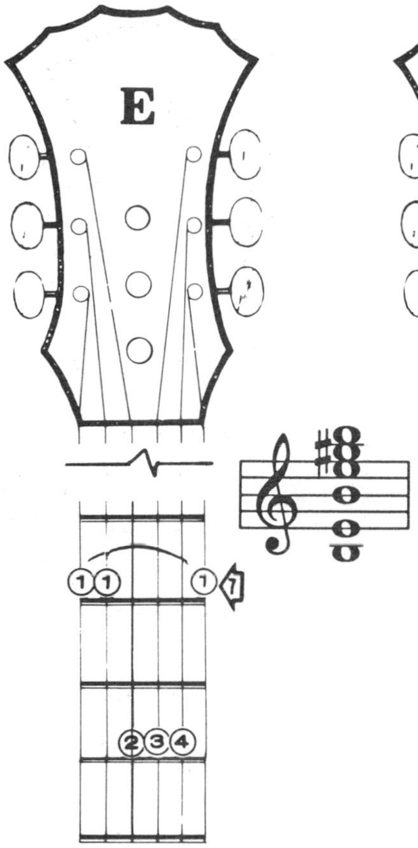

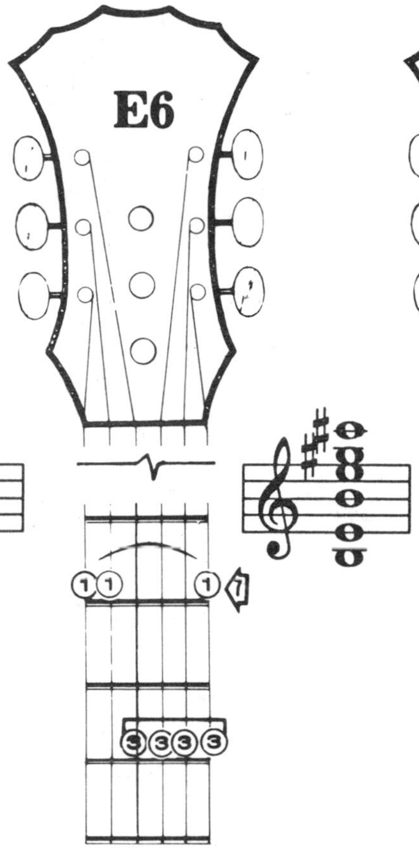

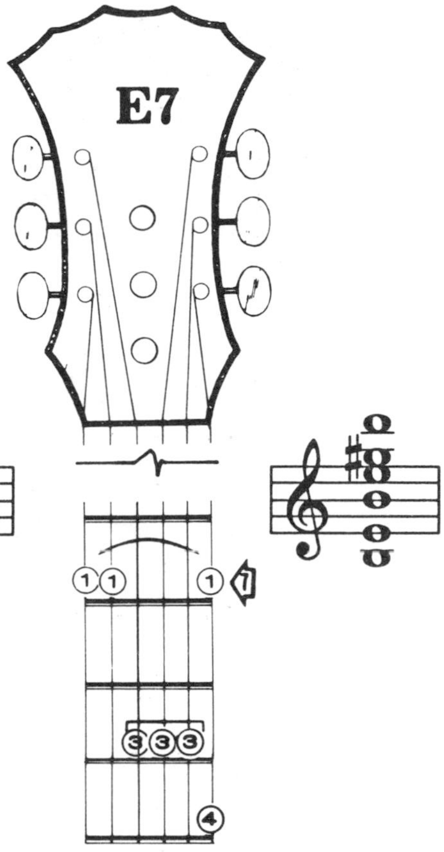

*Optional Fingering

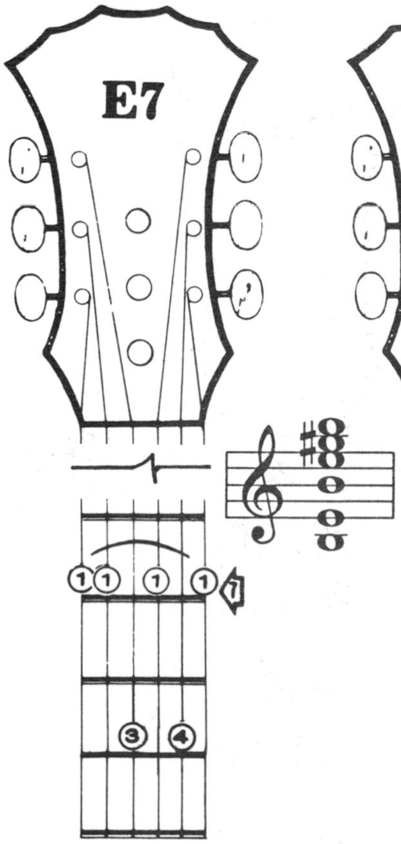

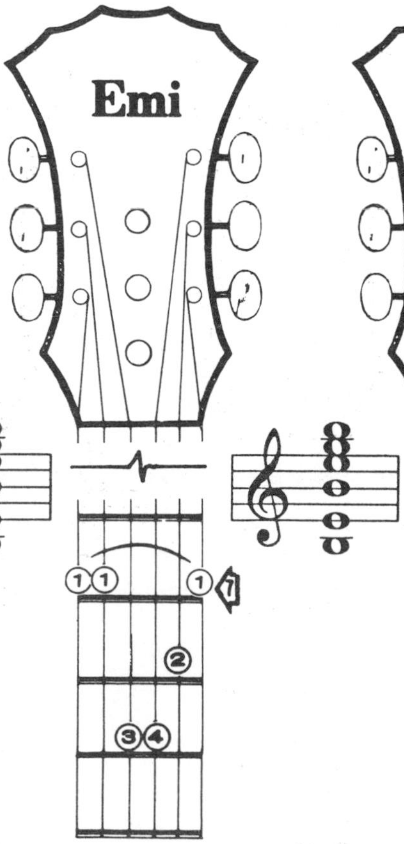

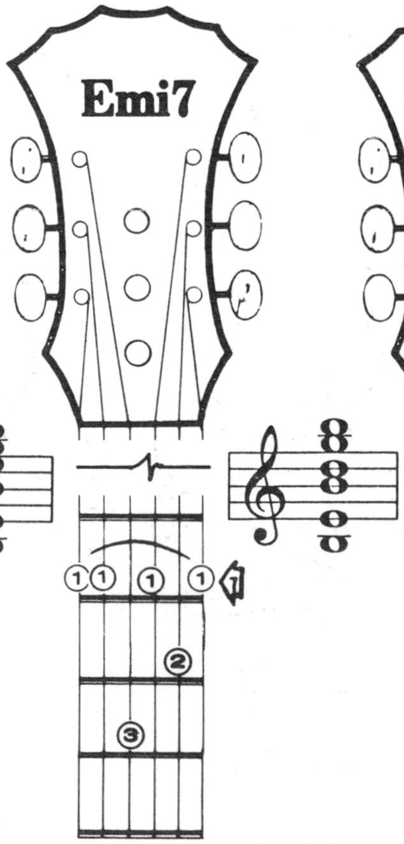

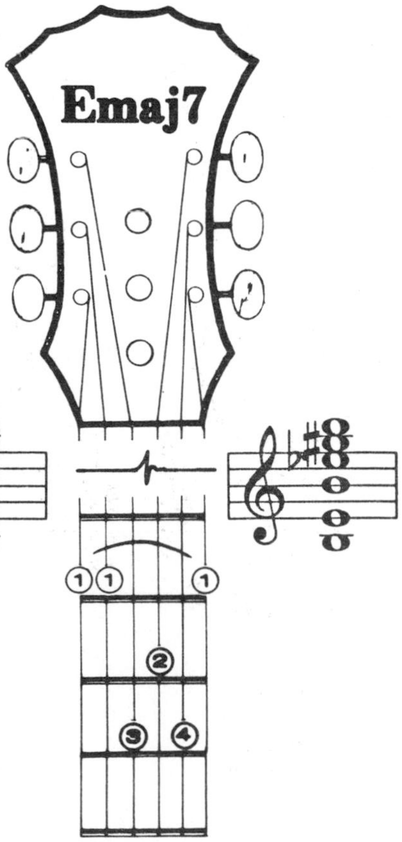

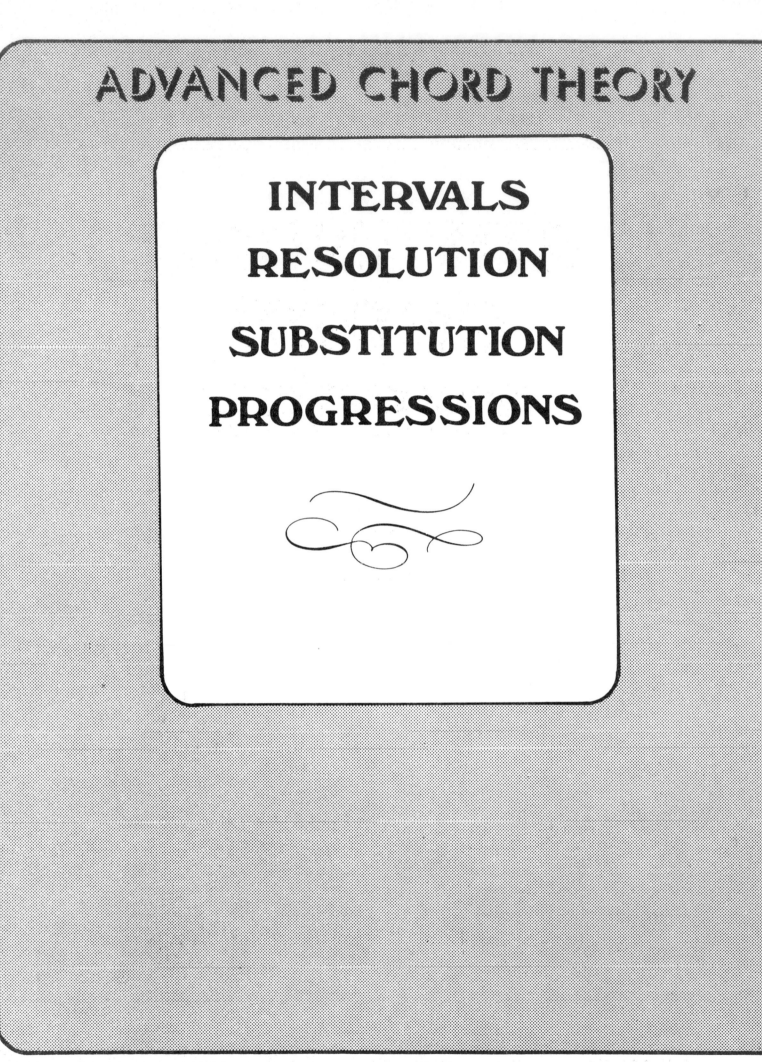

ADVANCED CHORD THEORY

INTERVALS
RESOLUTION
SUBSTITUTION
PROGRESSIONS

ADVANCED CHORD THEORY

ADVANCED CHORD THEORY

ADVANCED CHORD THEORY

INTERVALS

It becomes necessary to understand INTERVALS if the guitarist is interested in furthering his knowledge of chord construction. While the use of Intervals is normally confined to melody and harmony, they are important to us as the chord will normally be comprised of tones that harmonize with the melody. It is not within the scope of this book to teach the rudiments of harmony, however the basic knowledge of harmony along with an understanding of music terminology related to harmony will aid any guitarist.

An INTERVAL is the distance between two notes of a scale measured by whole and half steps. The lower tone is considered the Root or Key tone, and the upper tone is the INTERVAL. An Interval is the difference in pitch between the two tones when sounded.

MELODIC INTERVAL

When two tones of a different pitch, an Interval, are played in succession it is called a MELODIC INTERVAL, Illustration One.

HARMONIC INTERVAL

When two tones are played together as in a chord it is called a HARMONIC INTERVAL, Illustration One.

C SCALE—INTERVALS

There are five names given to intervals: *Major, Minor, Diminished, Augmented, and Perfect*. To enable the student to better understand the principles of intervals we have written the *C* scale, Illustration Two.

The first Interval is called the PRIME or UNISON Interval—two notes of the same letter name. PRIME: Two tones of the same pitch.

The second Interval is the distance between the first note, the letter *C* and the next note in the scale, the note *D*. The third Interval is the distance between the first note, *C* and the third note of the scale, the note *E*. The fourth Interval is the distance between the *C* and the fourth note of the scale, the note *F*. The fifth Interval is the distance between the *C* and the fifth note of the scale, the note *G*. The sixth Interval is the distance between the note *C* and the sixth note, the note *A*. The seventh Interval is the distance between the letter *C* and the seventh note of the scale, the note *B*. The last Interval is called the OCTAVE since the eighth note of the scale is of the same letter name as the first note, one octave apart.

PERFECT INTERVALS

When the INTERVAL is the Prime, fourth, fifth, or Octave, and the upper note is of the same scale as the lower note it is called a PERFECT INTERVAL, Illustration Four.

MAJOR INTERVALS

The second, third, sixth, and seventh INTERVALS are called MAJOR INTERVALS, Illustration Five.

MINOR INTERVALS

When the notes of a Major Interval are brought closer together, we have a MINOR Interval. This may be done by lowering the upper tone one half step, or raising the lower tone a half step. The Minor Interval applies only to Major Intervals—the second, third, sixth, and seventh tones.

DIMINISHED INTERVALS

The Diminished Interval is obtained by bringing a PERFECT Interval closer together, or a MINOR Interval closer together, lowering the Perfect or Minor Interval.

AUGMENTED INTERVALS

When the interval between two tones is EXPANDED, the interval is called AUGMENTED. This applies to both the Major and Perfect Intervals. Each of these become Augmented by: Raising the upper tone one half step, or lowering the lower tone one half step.

INTERVALS

TWO TYPES OF INTERVALS

1a MELODIC INTERVAL   **1b HARMONIC INTERVAL**

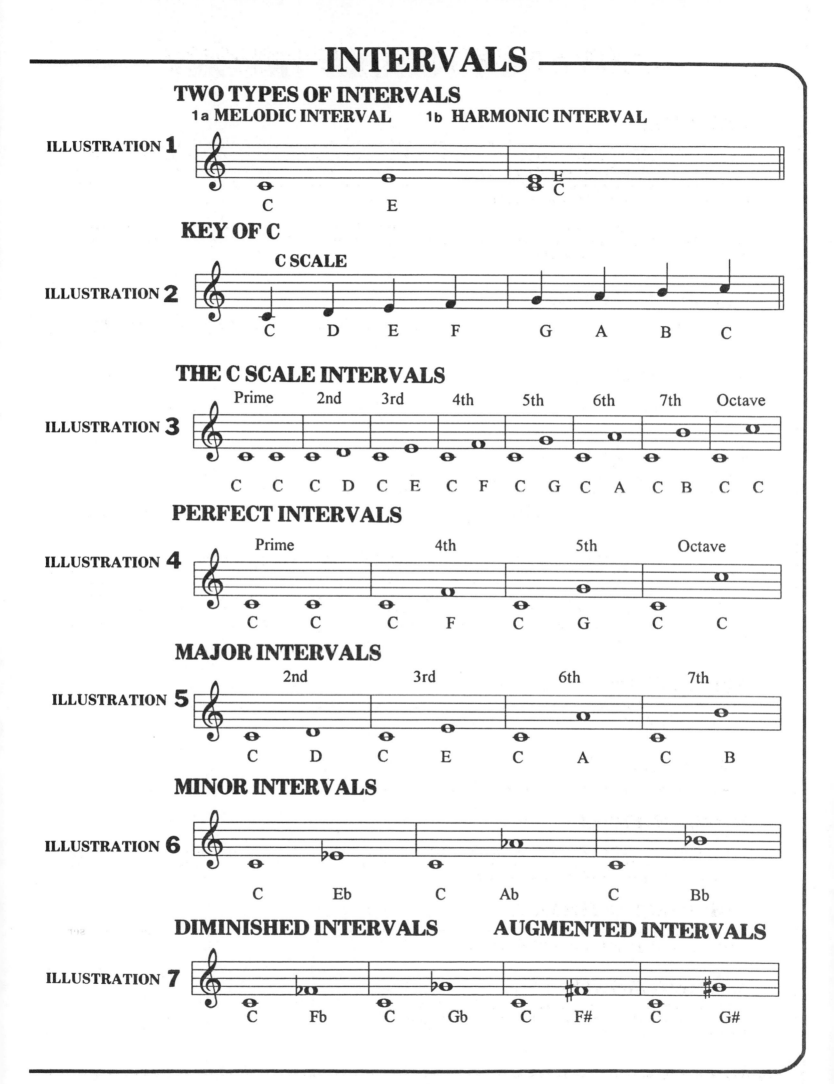

ILLUSTRATION 1

KEY OF C

ILLUSTRATION 2 — C SCALE — C D E F G A B C

THE C SCALE INTERVALS

ILLUSTRATION 3 — Prime, 2nd, 3rd, 4th, 5th, 6th, 7th, Octave

C C   C D   C E   C F   C G   C A   C B   C C

PERFECT INTERVALS

ILLUSTRATION 4 — Prime, 4th, 5th, Octave

C C   C F   C G   C C

MAJOR INTERVALS

ILLUSTRATION 5 — 2nd, 3rd, 6th, 7th

C D   C E   C A   C B

MINOR INTERVALS

ILLUSTRATION 6

C Eb   C Ab   C Bb

DIMINISHED INTERVALS   AUGMENTED INTERVALS

ILLUSTRATION 7

C Fb   C Gb   C F#   C G#

139

ADVANCED CHORD THEORY

MAJOR THIRDS

The term MAJOR 3rd will appear in most all chord books. This term is used in place of other related terminology in chord construction. It is only one more form of describing basic chords already explained in previous chapters in this book.

SEMI-TONE

A Semi-Tone is one half of a whole tone. It is the smallest interval in modern European music. A Semi-Tone is the distance of one fret on the guitar, Illustration One. Two Semi-Tones equal one whole tone, the distance of two frets on the guitar, Illustration One.

WHOLE STEP

The term—Step, Half Step, is another way of saying: Semi-Tone, Whole Tone. A whole tone is one step, the distance of two frets on the guitar, Illustration Two. A half step is the distance of one fret, or a Semi-Tone.

BUILDING A MAJOR THIRD

A Major 3rd interval is built on two whole tones, Illustration Three. In the C Scale a Major 3rd would be the distance from C to E. The notes C to D being one whole tone and D to E the other whole tone. In Illustration Four we show these three notes, C D and E. While the D note is not a part of the Major third interval, it is important in establishing the Major third intervals as three letters are used.

To better understand Major Thirds we have the Major third in written form showing how it appears on the staff, Illustration Five.

WHOLE TONES — SEMI TONES

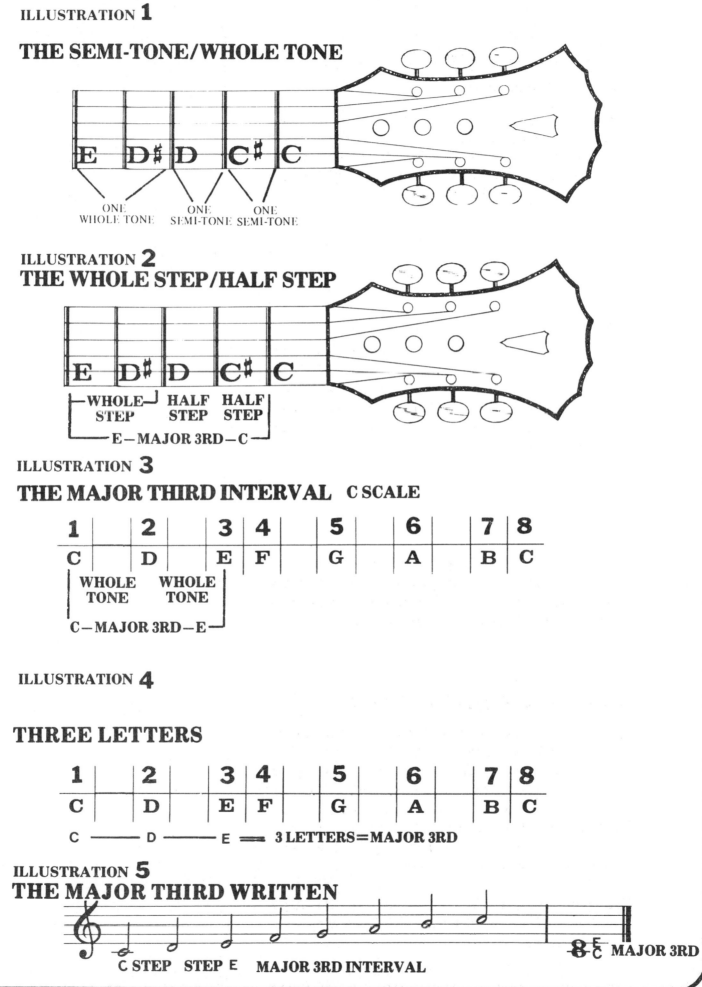

ILLUSTRATION **1**

THE SEMI-TONE/WHOLE TONE

E D♯ D C♯ C

ONE
WHOLE TONE

ONE
SEMI-TONE

ONE
SEMI-TONE

ILLUSTRATION **2**
THE WHOLE STEP/HALF STEP

E D♯ D C♯ C

WHOLE
STEP

HALF
STEP

HALF
STEP

E — MAJOR 3RD — C

ILLUSTRATION **3**

THE MAJOR THIRD INTERVAL C SCALE

1	2	3	4	5	6	7	8
C	D	E	F	G	A	B	C

WHOLE
TONE

WHOLE
TONE

C — MAJOR 3RD — E

ILLUSTRATION **4**

THREE LETTERS

1	2	3	4	5	6	7	8
C	D	E	F	G	A	B	C

C ——— D ——— E ══ 3 LETTERS = MAJOR 3RD

ILLUSTRATION **5**
THE MAJOR THIRD WRITTEN

C STEP   STEP E   MAJOR 3RD INTERVAL

E
C MAJOR 3RD

MINOR THIRDS

The MINOR Third is constructed on a whole tone, and a half tone, also called step, and half step. In Illustration One, we use the *C* Scale. From the note *C* to the note *D* is one whole tone, or one Step. From *D* we proceed a half step, or half tone to *E♭*. This is a Minor Third, from *C* to *E♭*. As in the Major 3rd, we are using three letters—*C D E♭*. Only here we have played a Step and a half, whereas a Major 3rd would be two full steps. Illustration Two shows this Minor 3rd built on the written scale.

THE MAJOR CHORD TRIAD

There are five chord types that the student must learn. They are: *Major, Minor, Diminished, Augmented, and Dominant 7th*. The Major chord is constructed on a Major 3rd and Minor 3rd interval, Illustration Three.

To construct a Major chord, we first build a Major 3rd interval, *C* to *E*, then on the higher note, the *E*, we build a Minor 3rd interval giving us the note *G*. Thus we have the Major chord triad for the *C* chord, *C E G*. In review we can state that a Major chord is constructed by building a Major 3rd and Minor 3rd interval.

THE WRITTEN MAJOR CHORD TRIAD

Illustration Four shows the notes as they appear on the written *C* Scale.

MAJOR — MINOR INTERVALS

ILLUSTRATION 1

THE MINOR THIRD INTERVAL

1		2	3	4		5		6		7	8
C		D	E♭	E	F		G		A		B	C

*WHOLE TONE HALF TONE ONE AND A HALF TONE — MINOR 3RD INTERVAL
*ALSO CALLED WHOLE STEP, HALF STEP

ILLUSTRATION 2

THE MINOR THIRD INTERVAL WRITTEN

C   E♭

ILLUSTRATION 3

THE MAJOR CHORD TRIAD

1		2		3	4		5		6		7	8
C		D		E	F	G♭	G		A		B	C

STEP   STEP   STEP   HALF STEP
MAJOR 3RD   MINOR 3RD   C CHORD = C E G

ILLUSTRATION 4

THE MAJOR CHORD TRIAD WRITTEN

C CHORD
TRIAD C E G

STEP   STEP   STEP   HALF STEP
MAJOR 3RD   MINOR 3RD

G
E
C

ADVANCED CHORD THEORY

MINOR CHORD TRIAD

Minor chords are constructed by combining a Minor 3rd interval with a Major 3rd. This lowers the Minor chord's third tone one Semi-Tone. When tones of a Major Interval are brought closer together we have a Minor Interval.

We still have three letters used in building the Minor Third— C Eb and G. The student should study Illustration One and thoroughly understand the principles of Major Thirds and Minor Thirds.

DIMINISHED CHORD TRIAD

The Diminished chord triad, unlike the Major, Minor and Augumented chord, is a four note chord. It is comprised of two Minor 3rds superimposed over each other. The Diminished chord is a very unstable chord and demands resolution to another chord.

There are four different Augumented chords, each spelled three different ways. (See basic chord theory.)

AUGMENTED CHORD TRIAD

The Augmented chord is constructed of two Major 3rds superimposed over each other. There is no true ROOT tone in an Augmented chord. As a result of this condition, there is an unsettled relationship between the Root and the 5th tone. The Augmented (raised 5th) tone, the notes C to $G\#$, eliminates the static quality of the chord and there is no single predominant tone as found in a Major chord.

There are three different Augmented chords, each spelled three different ways. (See basic chord theory.)

MAJOR SEVEN CHORD TRIAD

The Major Seventh chord is constructed of a Major 3rd, Minor 3rd, and a Major 3rd. The Major Seven Chord is a four tone chord and as the fourth note, the seventh note, is only a half step from the Root (1st) note of the chord triad, the Major Seventh chord is a stable chord and often used as a substitution for the Tonic Chord.

MINOR-AUGMENTED-DIMINISHED TRIADS

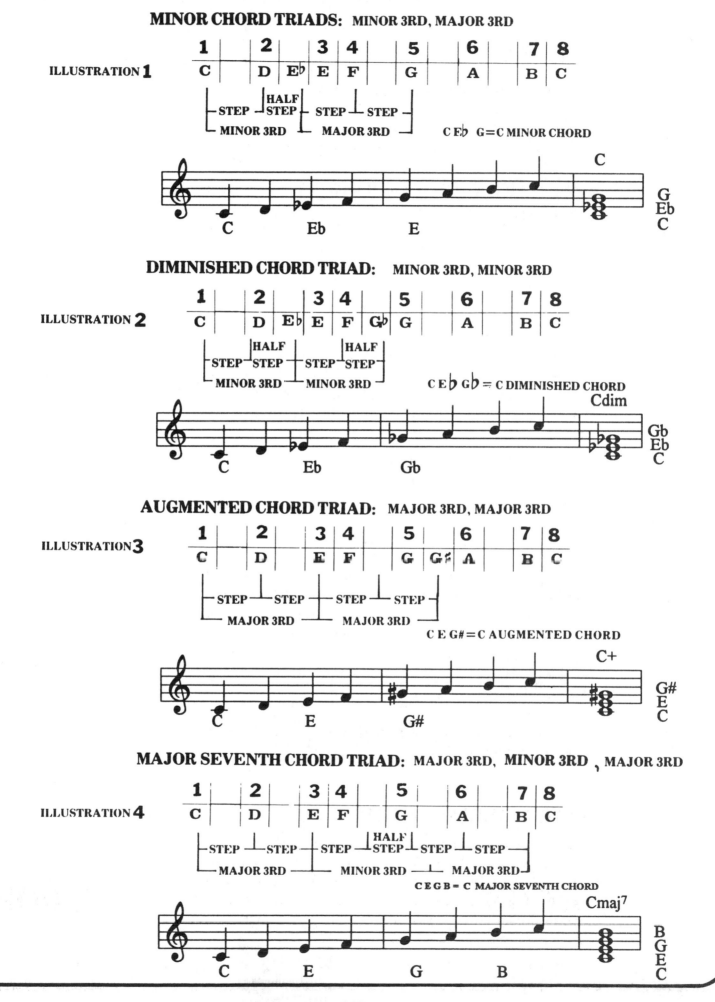

MINOR CHORD TRIADS: MINOR 3RD, MAJOR 3RD

ILLUSTRATION 1

DIMINISHED CHORD TRIAD: MINOR 3RD, MINOR 3RD

ILLUSTRATION 2

AUGMENTED CHORD TRIAD: MAJOR 3RD, MAJOR 3RD

ILLUSTRATION 3

MAJOR SEVENTH CHORD TRIAD: MAJOR 3RD, MINOR 3RD, MAJOR 3RD

ILLUSTRATION 4

ADVANCED CHORD THEORY

AUGMENTED RESOLUTION

If we were to build a series of Major 3rd intervals played one above the other, we would have the Augmented chord. The Augmented chord triad consists of the Root, Major 3rd, and an Augmented (raised) 5th, Illustration One.

The Augumented chord is a very active chord and will progress to the next chord in the cycle of Keys, moving through the Keys in a circle of 4ths, page 56. For example, the *G* Augumented chord will resolve to the *C* Chord, (*G*, *A*, *B*, *C*(. The *C* Augumented chord will resolve to the *F* chord, (*C*, *D*, *E*, *F*). Again, following the circle of 4ths.
The exercise in Illustration Two will give the student the opportunity to hear this resolution. For better chord voicing use the positions shown in Illustration Five.

DIMINISHED RESOLUTION

The Diminished chord is bulit on Minor third intervals, Illustration Three.

The Diminished chord may be used as a substitution for the Dominant 7th chord. There is strong inter-relationship between the tones of a Diminished chord which creates the impression that each note of the chord may be the Root tone, Actually, the Diminished chord has no Root tone.

The Diminished 7 chord offers many possibilities for the rhythm guitarists as it can be used to modulate to other new keys. Practice the chord progression shown in Illustration Four.

AUGMENTED — DIMINISHED RESOLUTION

ILLUSTRATION 1

AUGMENTED CHORD (R 3 #5)

Gaug—G+

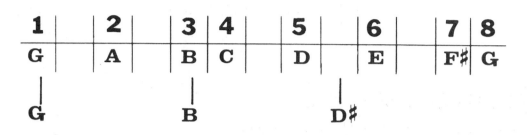

ILLUSTRATION 2

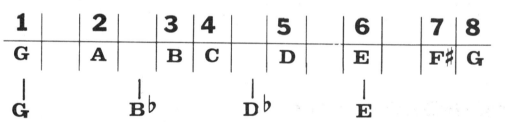

ILLUSTRATION 3

DIMINISHED CHORD (R ♭3 ♭5 6 (♭♭ 7)

Gdim—G°

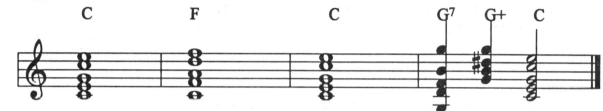

ILLUSTRATION 4

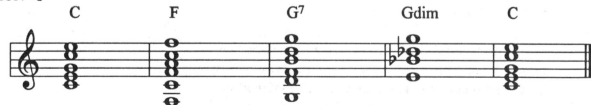

ILLUSTRATION 5   USE THE CHORD FINGERING SHOWN HERE

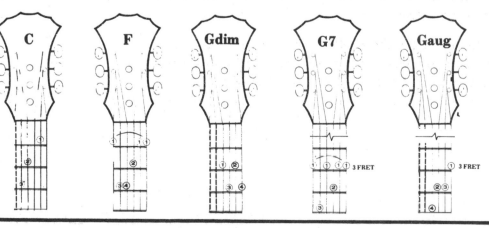

TONE RESOLUTION

"Chord Resolution": The tendency of chords to progress toward a point of rest. Perhaps you have already discovered that certain tones of the Major scale sound best when they "Resolve" (move to some other tone within the scale). For example, in our chord cycles, the Dominant chord sounds complete only when we return to the Tonic chord.

The Diatonic Scale is comprised of seven tones, with the eighth tone repeating the first, an octave higher. Some of the tones are static and sound complete in them- selves. Others never sound complete and usually resolve to other tones to become complete. The seven tones in the scale are divided into "Active Tones" demand- ing resolution, and "Inactive Tones" complete in themselves.

In Illustration One we have diagramed, horizontally, the *C* Diatonic Scale, num- bering each degree. Directly below each letter we have the proper theoritical names of the degrees. Then we have the written scale indicating which tones are Active and Inactive.

ACTIVE TONES: 2, 4, 6, and 7. INACTIVE TONES: 1, 3, and 5.

TONE RESOLUTION

To demonstrate the tendencies of Active tones to resolve to Inactive ones, play the simple progression shown in Illustration Two.

Play the progression through once and then start through again stopping on different chords, such as the Sub-Dominant. Listen to the unsettled tone created. You ear will tell you that you should not rest on the Sub-Dominant chord.

Any chord played during the course of a cycle demands some kind of temporary resolution until it eventually reaches the Tonic tone again. For this reason most songs will end on the Tonic (Key) chord. Ending on any other chord will leave the listener waiting, unsettled.

DOMINANT SEVENTH CHORD

While the Dominant tone is an *inactive* tone, the addition of the *seventh* tone (flatted seventh) dramatically changed the normal resolution of the dominant chord to a very active chord.

The seventh tone is called a *leading tone* and this will definitely change the inactive dominant chord to an active chord demanding resolution to the tonic tone.

ACTIVE-INACTIVE TONES

The active tones as previously stated will resolve to other tones in the scale, and we know the general movement of the tones. Normally the best sounding movements are as follows:

The strongest resolution of the Supertonic (2) is down to the Tonic (1).
The strongest resolution of the Submediant (6) is down to the Dominant (5).
The strongest resolution of the Subdominant (4) is up to the Dominant (5).
The strongest resolution of all active tones is the Leading Tone (7) to the Tonic (1), or Octave Tone (8).

CHORD RESOLUTION
ACTIVE—INACTIVE TONES

ILLUSTRATION 1

ACTIVE/INACTIVE TONES

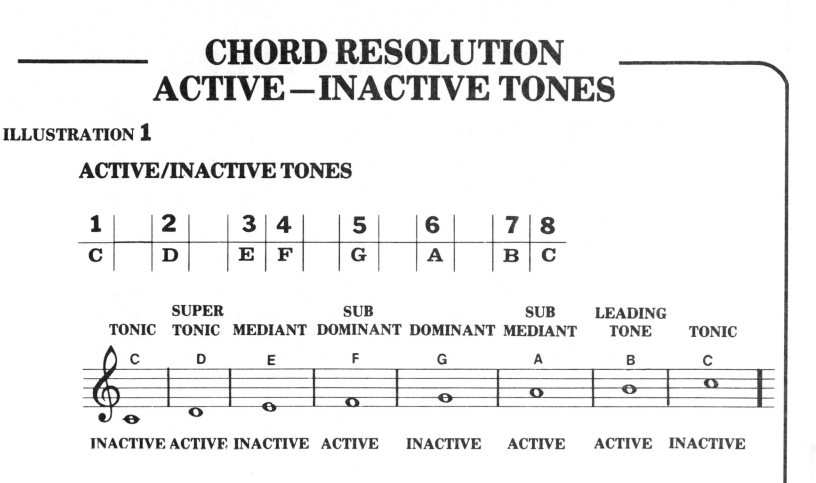

ILLUSTRATION 2

A BASIC CHORD PROGRESSION (KEY OF C)

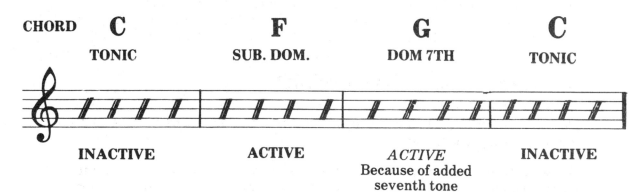

RESOLUTION:

RESOLUTION: The tendency of chords to progress toward a point of rest.

THE DOMINANT 7 CHORD RESOLUTION

The Tonic chord is the most important chord in music composition since most songs will start and end on the Tonic chord. The second most important chord is built on the DOMINANT tone of the scale, the fifth tone, or the V chord, Illustrations One and Two.

The Dominant 7 chord has four tones, unlike our three tone Triad R 3 5. This four tone chord is called a TETRIAD, and is built on the Root 3 5 ♭7, Illustrations Two and Three.

The Dominant 7 chord creates a sense of movement, a feeling of tension that wants to be resolved, and will always move back to the Tonic chord.

Practice playing the chords in Illustration Four using the Dominant 7. NOTE: The last chord, the Tonic F has been changed to an *F* Minor. This creates a different voicing and is acceptable, as it is "Direct Substitution" explained elsewhere in this book.

DOMINANT SEVENTH RESOLUTION

ILLUSTRATION 1

RESOLUTION OF THE DOMINANT SEVENTH

DOM 7 R 3 5 ♭7

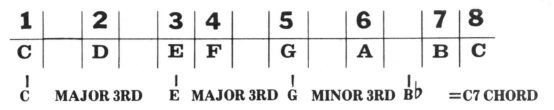

1		2		3	4		5		6		7	8
C		D		E	F		G		A		B	C

C — MAJOR 3RD — E — MAJOR 3RD — G — MINOR 3RD — B♭ — = C7 CHORD

ILLUSTRATION 2

C   E   G   B♭

ILLUSTRATION 3

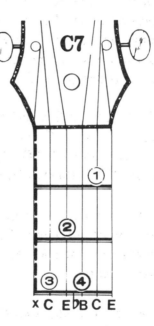

ILLUSTRATION 4

DOMINANT SEVENTH RESOLUTION

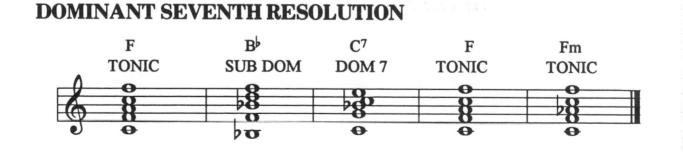

F	B♭	C7	F	Fm
TONIC	SUB DOM	DOM 7	TONIC	TONIC

RESOLUTION OF THE DOMINANT 7

Although there are various ways to play chord progressions, the student should always remember that no matter how many chords are added to a chord progression, they should eventually reach the Dominant 7 chord and from there resolve to the Tonic chord.

Illustration One is an exercise in chord resolution. In the first Illustration, One A, we have a very simple resolution of the tonic chord to the Dominant 7 and back to the Tonic again. To achieve a better tonal progression we can add additional chords, Illustration One B. When the chord movement resolves directly from the Tonic to the Dominant 7, or from the Dominant 7 to the Tonic, we can insert the Supertonic II chord. Also it is possible to use the II chord in place of the Dominant 7 chord and resolve into the Dominant chord from the II chord.

RESOLUTION USING THE II CHORD

The Supertonic, II chord, is a secondary Triad, a Minor chord. (See Scale of Triads.) The best progression of the II chord is to the Dominant 7. Because the II chord is very similar to the IV chord (one note's difference) a pleasant sounding progression can be created by playing the IV to II to the V (Dominant 7th) chord. Study the exercises in Illustration Two. We show the proper fingering for each chord.

TONIC TO DOMINANT

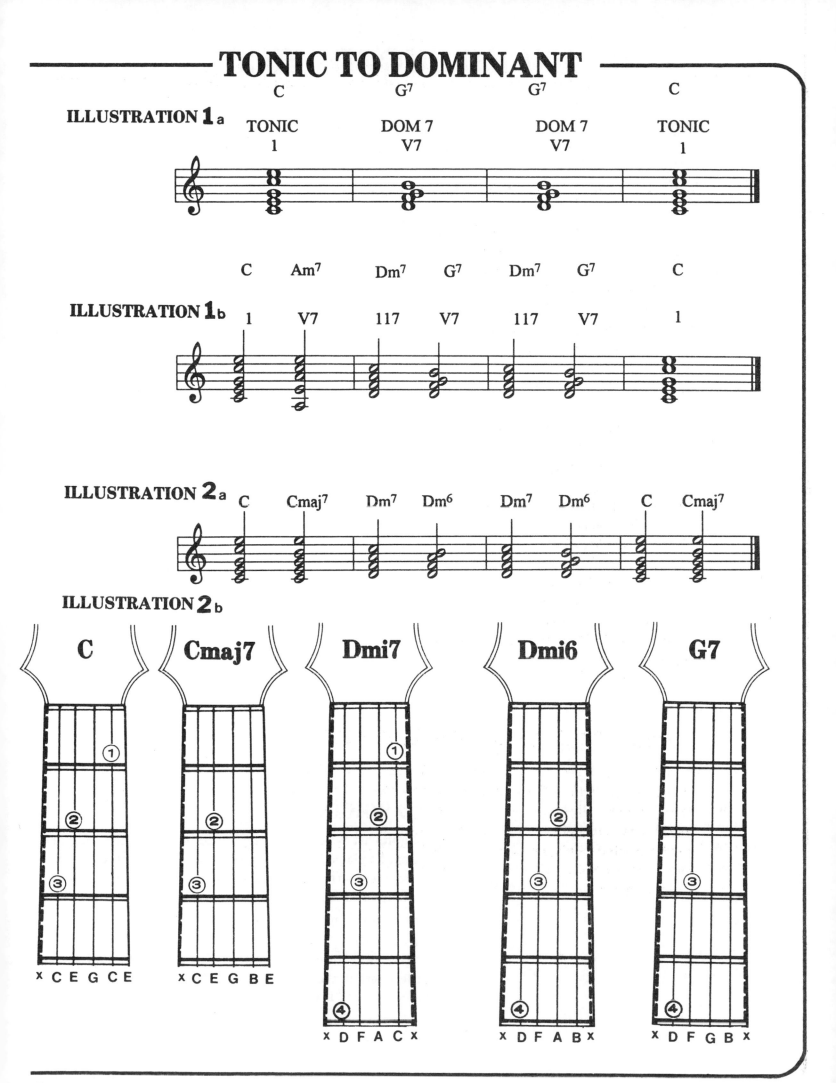

ILLUSTRATION 1a

C	G⁷	G⁷	C
TONIC	DOM 7	DOM 7	TONIC
1	V7	V7	1

ILLUSTRATION 1b

C	Am⁷	Dm⁷	G⁷	Dm⁷	G⁷	C
1	V7	117	V7	117	V7	1

ILLUSTRATION 2a

C Cmaj⁷ Dm⁷ Dm⁶ Dm⁷ Dm⁶ C Cmaj⁷

ILLUSTRATION 2b

C — x C E G C E

Cmaj7 — x C E G B E

Dmi7 — x D F A C x

Dmi6 — x D F A B x

G7 — x D F G B x

153

THE SUSPENDED CHORD

The SUSPENDED chord is one in which the third of the chord triad is raised one half step. This changes the Triad from R 3 5 to R 4 5, Illustration One. In Illustration Two we show how this can be put into practical usage. We have changed the C chord, C E G Triad to C Sus chord, C F G Triad.

The Suspended chord is commonly written as Csus. In discussing the Suspended chord you may encounter such terms as: Augmented 3rd, Raised 3rd. Both of these terms are used to imply raising the third tone of the chord Triad one half step.

The Suspended tone is also referred to as a NON HARMONIC tone as it has a dissonant sound that demands resolution. Usually the Suspended chord will resolve to the Dominant 7th of the same name. As an example the C Sus resolves to the C7, the G Sus will resolve to the G7 chord.

DOMINANT 7 SUSPENDED CHORD A MOVABLE CHORD

The Dominant 7 Sus chord can be a movable chord by eliminating the unfretted string as shown in Illustrations Two and Three. The Root note will be on the second string. Following the Chromatic Scale, Illustration Five, you will be able to play twelve Suspended chords with each position shown.

CHORD VOICING

The good guitarist is constantly trying to improve each song or arrangement he plays. Every song requires a different approach in order to create the best possible feeling or mood. Chord voicing will determine how well this is accomplished.

The term chord voicing implies TONE COLORING.

Play the two Sus chords, Illustrations Two and Four. Listen to the differences in the sound created. This is "Tone Coloring". What will sound well in one arrangement may not fit in another.

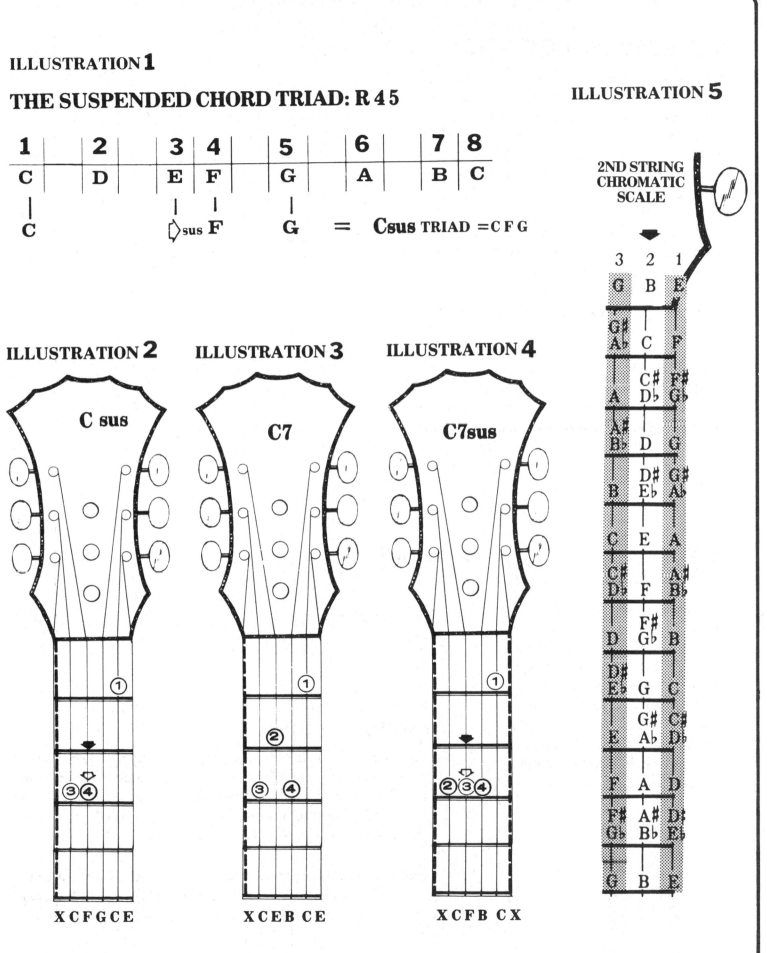

ILLUSTRATION 1

THE SUSPENDED CHORD TRIAD: R 4 5

ILLUSTRATION 5

1	2	3	4	5	6	7	8
C	D	E	F	G	A	B	C

C   ⬦sus F   G   =   **Csus** TRIAD = C F G

2ND STRING
CHROMATIC
SCALE

ILLUSTRATION 2   **ILLUSTRATION 3**   **ILLUSTRATION 4**

C sus   C7   C7sus

X C F G C E   X C E B C E   X C F B C X

ADVANCED CHORD THEORY

CHORD SUBSTITUTION

If you have listened to the great Jazz guitarists you know the degree of skill these guitarists have developed in creating new and original rhythmic chord progressions. A good Jazz man can take a simple melody or lead line and build a never-ending improvised arrangement from it.

They can spend hours playing complex chord progressions without repeating the same chord pattern twice. To accomplish this they use their knowledge of chord substitution. The theory of chord substitution can be as simple as learning to add 6th, 7th or 9th notes to chords, or as complex as to require a lifetime of study in music theory, harmony chord construction, plus extensive ear training.

One advantage of utilizing chord substitution is that simple chord progression can be played without the monotonous repetition of using the same chords measure after measure. Since there are many chords that can be used in place of any given chord, repetition can be avoided and new, original and interesting chord progressions created.

Chord substitution can be accomplished by applying different rules of substitution, such as will be shown on the following pages. These include: Direct Substitution, The Flatted 5th Substitution, The 5th Higher Substitution, Scalewise Substitution, Minor Chord for Dominant 7 Chord Substitution, and the Rule of Common Tone. At first the student studying chord substitution can be completely overwhelmed at the complexities involved, however the student should always remember that sound, basic laws of music are always being applied. The better you understand these laws the easier it is to understand how the professional is able to achieve the chord progressions used today.

DIRECT CHORD SUBSTITUTION

Every chord has two names: LETTER NAME and TYPE NAME. The LETTER NAME may be any letter of the musical alphabet and may be either "Sharped" or "Flatted". Example: *A B C D E F G*, or *A# B♭* etc. The chord Type name can be MAJOR, MINOR, DOMINANT, AUGMENTED and DIMINISHED. As a result we have chords like: *Gmaj7, Cmi, A7, Ddim, Faug*, etc.

When a MAJOR chord is used in an arrangement, we may use in its place any MAJOR type chord of the same LETTER name. Example: If the original chord is *G*, we could substitute *G6*, *G9*, *G13*, etc. By substituting a like name chord for another like name chord we have DIRECT SUBSTITUTION.

USING MINOR CHORDS

The MINOR chord may be used as a substitute for a MAJOR chord of the same LETTER NAME. Example: original chord *G*—Substitution chord—*Gmi, Gmi6, Gmi9*, etc. Again—Like name chord for like name chord—DIRECT SUBSTITUTION.

CHORD SUBSTITUTION

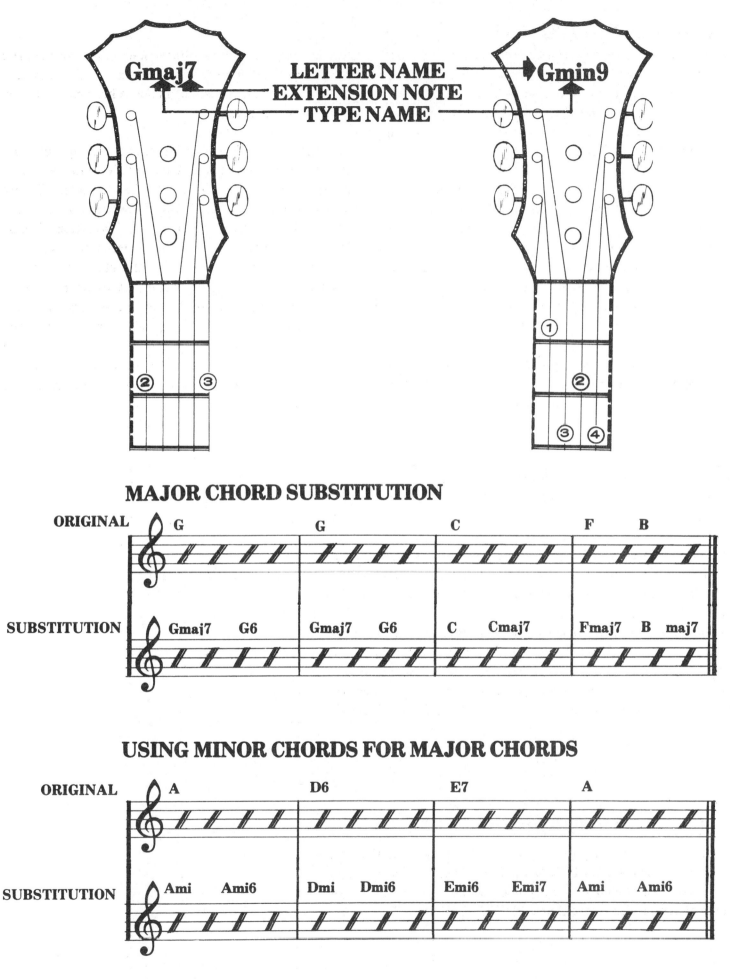

Gmaj7

LETTER NAME
EXTENSION NOTE
TYPE NAME

Gmin9

MAJOR CHORD SUBSTITUTION

ORIGINAL

G	G	C	F B

SUBSTITUTION

Gmaj7 G6	Gmaj7 G6	C Cmaj7	Fmaj7 B maj7

USING MINOR CHORDS FOR MAJOR CHORDS

ORIGINAL

A	D6	E7	A

SUBSTITUTION

Ami Ami6	Dmi Dmi6	Emi6 Emi7	Ami Ami6

ADVANCED CHORD THEORY

MINOR CHORD SUBSTITUTION

It is permissible to use several types of Minor chord substitutions when a Minor chord appears in a chord progression.

DIRECT SUBSTITUTION

When a Minor type chord is used in a song we may, by direct substitution, play any Minor type chord such as: Minor 6th, Minor 7th, Minor 9th, etc.

MAJOR CHORD FOR MINOR CHORD

Any major chord of the same letter name as the original minor chord may be used as a form of direct substitution.

DOMINANT 7TH A 5TH HIGHER

Another Minor chord substitution that is frequently used, although care must be exercised in order not to create dissonant tonal coloring against the melody, is the DOMINANT 7th a 5th HIGHER.

When a Minor chord appears in a chord progression we can count up a fifth interval and substitute a Dominant type chord. Actually it is easier to understand it this way—When a Minor chord is used and you want to substitute a new chord, write out the Minor chord triad (R $\flat$ 3 5), we do this so we may determine the Minor chord's 5th interval. Example: The *G* Minor chord would be *G B $\flat$ D*, the 5th of the triad being the note *D*. We then would build a Dominant chord on the *D* note and play any *D* Dominant chord we desire.

CHORD SUBSTITUTION

MINOR CHORDS FOR MINOR CHORDS

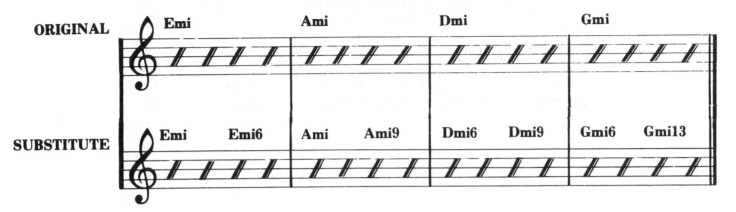

MAJOR CHORDS FOR MINOR CHORDS

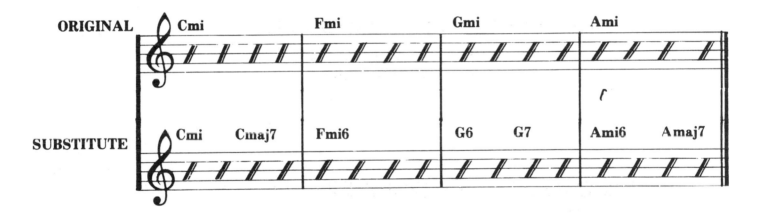

DOMINANT 7 A 5TH HIGHER

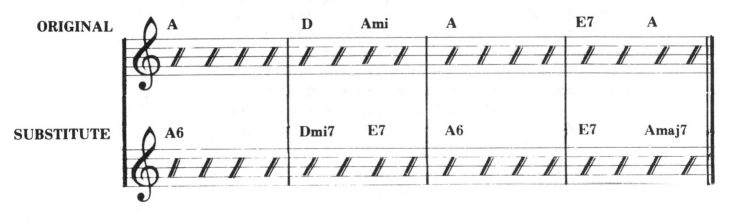

ASCENDING SCALE PROGRESSION
UP TO THE THIRD DEGREE

The rule of ASCENDING SCALE PROGRESSION as a substitute for Major chords should be studied in detail. Not only can a direct substitution be made for Major chords, but a colorful tonal movement created.

When a Major chord is used in a chord progression it is permissible to play a scalewise chord progression up to the third degree of the scale.

Chords built upon the Tonic or first note of the scale are Major chords, chords built upon the Supertonic and the Mediant, the second and third notes of the scale, played as Minor chords, Illustration One.

We must use the Diatonic Scale of the letter name of each Major chord to establish the three proper chords for substition. In other words each time a Major chord appears in a progression and we want to substitute a scalewise progression, we must start with the first chord as our Tonic chord and then establish the Second and Third chords from its Diatonic Scale. Practice the Scalewise Progression up to the 3rd degree as shown in Illustration Two.

DESCENDING SCALE PROGRESSION

It is also common practice to use the Scalewise progression out of descending scalewise order. Study the examples in Illustration Three and be sure you understand how each chord substitution was achieved.

SCALEWISE PROGRESSION USED
AS A MAJOR CHORD SUBSTITUTION

ILLUSTRATION 1

ASCENDING PROGRESSION
UP TO THE THIRD DEGREE

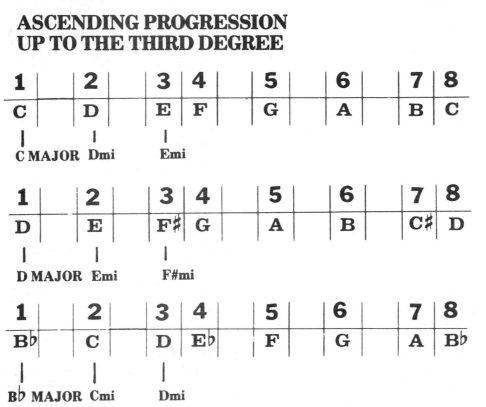

1	2	3	4	5	6	7	8
C	D	E	F	G	A	B	C

C MAJOR   Dmi   Emi

1	2	3	4	5	6	7	8
D	E	F#	G	A	B	C#	D

D MAJOR   Emi   F#mi

1	2	3	4	5	6	7	8
Bb	C	D	Eb	F	G	A	Bb

Bb MAJOR   Cmi   Dmi

ILLUSTRATION 2

SCALEWISE PROGRESSION UP TO THE THIRD DEGREE

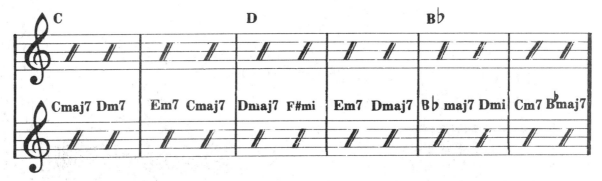

Cmaj7 Dm7 | Em7 Cmaj7 | Dmaj7 F#mi | Em7 Dmaj7 | Bb maj7 Dmi | Cm7 Bbmaj7

ILLUSTRATION 3

DESCENDING SCALE PROGRESSION

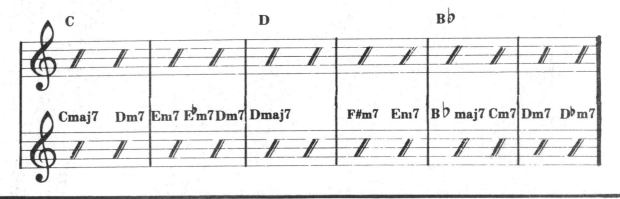

Cmaj7   Dm7 Em7 Ebm7 Dm7 Dmaj7   F#m7 Em7 Bb maj7 Cm7 Dm7 Dbm7

161

ASCENDING PROGRESSION
ONLY UP TO THE SECOND DEGREE

While we can use the Scalewise Progression up to the 3rd degree of the Diatonic Scale, it is not always necessary to do so. It is permissible to use the Scalewise Progression only as high as the 2nd degree of the scale, Illustration One.

ASCENDING PROGRESSION
UP TO THE FOURTH DEGREE

There are times when it is permissible to play the Scalewise Progression up to the 4th degree of the scale, and the chords formed on the 4th degree may be either Major or Minor, depending which sounds best in the tonal movement, Illustration Two.

DESCENDING PROGRESSION
IN "HALF STEPS"

We can also use the scalewise Major chord substitution in descending HALF STEPS. When descending from the 3rd degree it is permissible to descend by half steps. When a chord is one tone lower than the first chord and of the exact same letter name and type, we can descend in half steps, Illustration Three.

ASCENDING SCALEWISE PROGRESSION
AS A MAJOR CHORD SUBSTITUTION

ILLUSTRATION 1

ASCENDING PROGRESSION
ONLY TO THE SECOND DEGREE

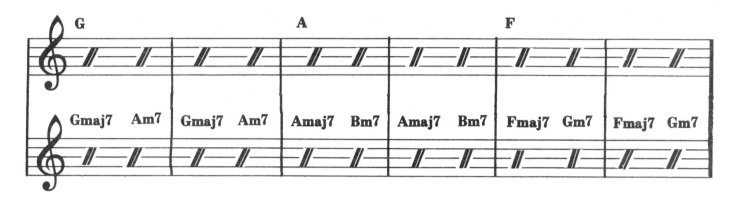

ILLUSTRATION 2

ASCENDING PROGRESSION
UP TO THE 4TH DEGREE

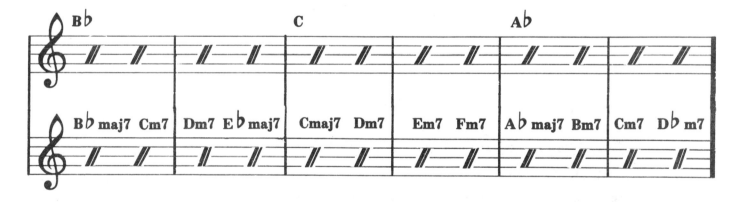

ILLUSTRATION 3

DESCENDING PROGRESSION
IN "HALF STEPS"

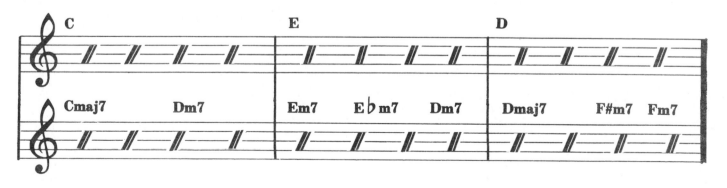

ADVANCED CHORD THEORY

DOMINANT 7TH SUBSTITUTION

There are three acceptable ways to apply chord substitution to the Dominant 7 chord. They are: "Direct Substitution," "Dominant Substitution a ♭5th higher," and "Minor Substitution a 5th Interval Higher." A thorough understanding of these principles of chord substitution is required to effectively create original chord progressions, as the Dominant 7 chord has the strongest resolution to the Tonic chord, resolving back to the Tonic chord.

DIRECT SUBSTITUTION

When a Dominant 7th chord appears we may substitute any Dominant 7 type chord of the same LETTER name as the original chord. This is called DIRECT SUBSTITUTION and the student must fully understand the various types of Dominant chords that may be used. We may alter the basic triad or extend it by adding additional notes to it. The Dominant chord Triad is: R 3 5 ♭7.

Chords such as the Dominant 7#9, the Dominant 7 ♭9, Illustration Three, are examples of chords that may be directly substituted for the Dominant 7 chord since they are all basically Dominant 7 type chords, Illustrations One and Two.

CHORD VOICING

Special attention must be given to proper chord voicing. In Illustration Three the *G7#9*, and the *B7♭9* are formed at the 8th fret, thusly, the *C* and *F* chords should also be played within this position on the neck. NOTE: The Augmented chord is a Major type chord and can be used as a DIRECT substitution for Major chords having the same LETTER name, however, only an Augmented 7 can be used as a substitute for a Dominant 7 chord.

SUBSTITUTION FOR THE DOMINANT 7TH

ILLUSTRATION 1

DIRECT SUBSTITUTION

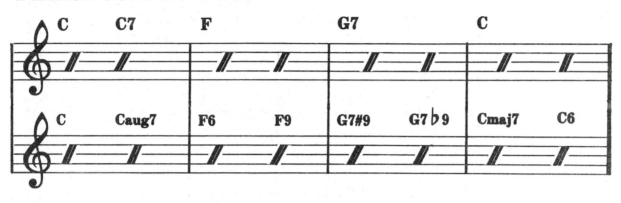

ILLUSTRATION 2

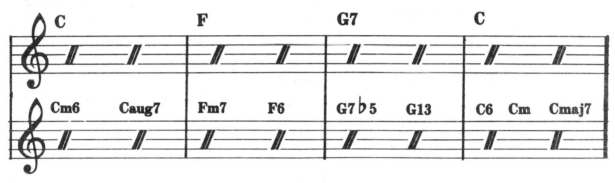

ILLUSTRATION 3

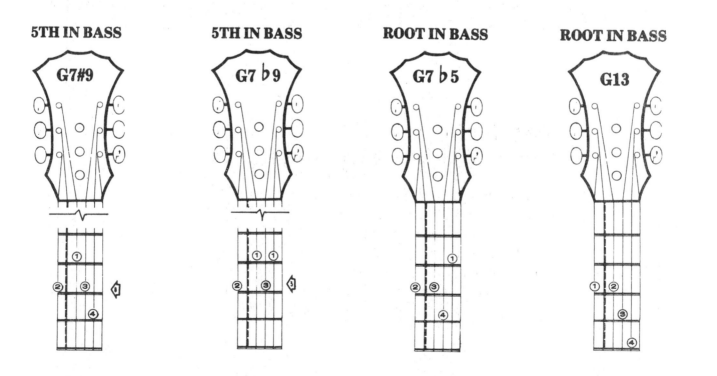

ADVANCED CHORD THEORY

DOMINANT 7 SUBSTITUTION USING THE MINOR CHORD A 5TH HIGHER

When a Dominant 7 chord appears we may substitute a Minor type chord built on the 5th note of the original chord triad. Any Minor type chord may be used: Minor 9, Minor 6, Minor 7, etc.

THE TERMS: 5TH INTERVAL AND 5TH HIGHER

This substitution rule may also be referred to as the "5th Interval, 5th Interval Higher" substitution. Since you may not always know the original chords triad, the same information may be obtained by merely counting up five notes from the chord "Letter" name. The *E7* chord, first letter *E*, five up, the letter *B*, Illustration One.

ILLUSTRATION ONE

The *E* Diatonic Scale has been used to show how the Minor 5th substitution should be used with the *E7* chord.

The 5th of the *E7* chord triad is the note *B*. Applying the rule of the 5th, we could use any *B* Minor type chord in place of the *E7* chord.

ILLUSTRATION TWO

The top line represents a standard chord progression using Dominant seventh chords. In the bottom line we have applied the Rule of the 5th, and created an entirely new family of chords in substitution of the original progression (top line).

ILLUSTRATION THREE

To aid you in practicing the chord progression shown in Illustration Two use the chord fingerings shown here.

DOMINANT 7TH SUBSTITUTION

ILLUSTRATION 1

USING THE MINOR CHORD A "FIFTH" HIGHER

E MAJOR DIATONIC SCALE

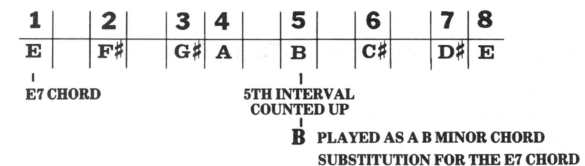

1	2	3	4	5	6	7	8
E	F#	G#	A	B	C#	D#	E

E7 CHORD

5TH INTERVAL
COUNTED UP

B PLAYED AS A B MINOR CHORD
SUBSTITUTION FOR THE E7 CHORD

ILLUSTRATION 2

ORIGINAL

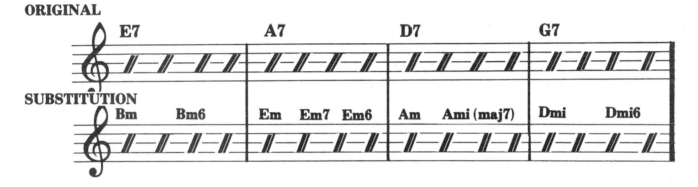

| E7 | A7 | D7 | G7 |

SUBSTITUTION

| Bm | Bm6 | Em | Em7 | Em6 | Am | Ami (maj7) | Dmi | Dmi6 |

ILLUSTRATION 3

CHORD VOICING

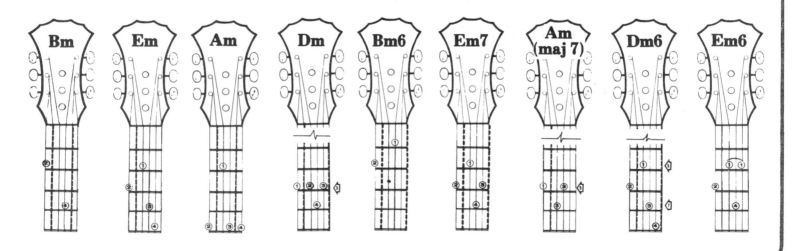

Bm Em Am Dm Bm6 Em7 Am (maj 7) Dm6 Em6

FLATTED 5TH SUBSTITUTION FOR THE DOMINANT SEVENTH

When a Dominant chord appears in a chord progression we may substitute any Major, Minor, or Seventh type chord built upon the FLATTED 5th of the original chord Triad.

Example: The *C7* chord Triad is—*C E G B♭*, Illustration One, the *C7* chord. The 5th of the *C7* chord Triad is the note *G*. By applying our flatted 5th rule, we would lower the *G* note to *G♭* and play a *G♭ 7*, or any other *G♭* type chord in substitution for the original chord.

CHORD PROGRESSION USING THE ♭5TH CHORD

In Illustration Two we show a standard chord progression as might be utilized in popular music. In the substitution line we have applied the Flatted 5th rule and changed the chord movement substantially. We can also use extended chords such as the *B+7*, *E13* and *B ♭9* chords.

CHORD VOICING

Practice playing the chord progression shown in Illustration Two using the chord fingerings (chord voicing) shown in Illustration Three.

SUBSTITUTION FOR THE DOMINANT 7TH
RULE OF THE FLATTED 5TH

ILLUSTRATION 1

FINDING THE FLATTED FIFTH

C SCALE   C7 CHORD

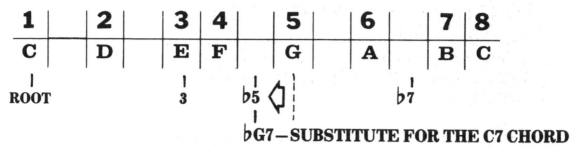

♭G7 — SUBSTITUTE FOR THE C7 CHORD

ILLUSTRATION 2

CHORD PROGRESSION USING THE ♭5TH CHORD

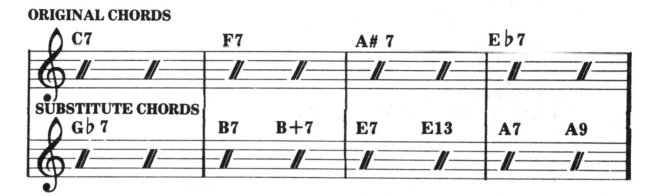

ILLUSTRATION 3

CHORD VOICING

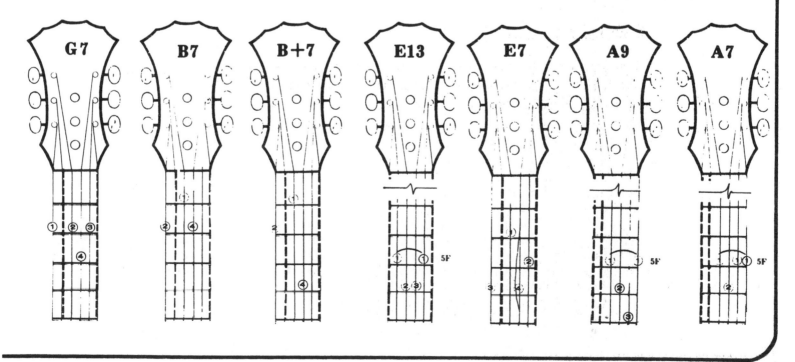

ADVANCED CHORD THEORY

ALTERED CHORDS

The term ALTERED CHORD is used to describe those chords built on the Diatonic Scale that have been "altered" (changed) by raising, or lowering a half step, one or more of the notes that comprise the chord triad; the Root, 3rd, 5th. This changes one or more notes in the chord to a note not in the original Key.

Jazz musicians love to take a simple melody and "do things" to it. They have learned how to give a song NEW color by employing what is known as FORCED HARMONY. This is simply a method of changing the type of chords used, or adding additional chords to standard chord progressions. This enables the player to move the harmonic melody away from, and back to, the Tonic chord again. This keeps the music active and always changing.

In modern Jazz it is important to know and understand CHORD SUBSTITUTION, a subject covered in detail previously. It is also necessary to understand how chords can be "altered" since altered chords are used extensively as substitute chords.

Since altered chords are commonly used in chord substitution, and as most chord melodies will eventually resolve to the Dominant chord before returning to the Tonic chord, it is desirable to know as many versions of the Dominant chord as possible.

THE DOMINANT 7 ♭5 CHORD

The Dominant 7 ♭5 chord is a Dominant seven chord with the fifth of the chord triad lowered one half step (one fret). Illustration One shows the standard $G7$ chord with the Root note in the bass, as used in Jazz progressions.

In Illustration Two the 5th, note D, has been lowered to $D♭$, changing the $G7$ chord to $G7♭5$.

THE DOMINANT 7+5

By raising the 5th of the triad one half step (one fret), we have changed the $G7$ chord to $G7+5$, Illustration Three.

ALTERED 5TH TONAL MOVEMENT

In this chord form the tonal movement, the flatting and raising of the 5th, takes place on the second string where the 5th of the chord triad, the note D is located.

A MOVABLE CHORD

This chord form is a MOVABLE CHORD as there are no open strings used in playing the chord. Since the Root note is on the sixth string, use the sixth string Chromatic Scale to determine the chord's name at each fret.

EXTENDED CHORDS

Chords may be extended by enlarging them beyond the seventh note, the DOMINANT SEVEN, to either the MAJOR SEVEN, the NINTH, ELEVENTH, or THIRTEENTH. Illustration Five shows the correct fingering for the $G13$ chord, an example of an EXTENDED chord. In this chord form the 5th of the chord triad has been raised two frets, one Whole Tone. Since this is also the sixth note of the scale, this chord is sometimes called a DOMINANT 7 add 6.

ALTERED CHORDS — EXTENDED CHORDS

ILLUSTRATION 1 — G7

ILLUSTRATION 2 — G7 ♭5

ILLUSTRATION 3 — G7+5

ILLUSTRATION 5 — G13

ILLUSTRATION 4

G7 = G B D F

G7 5 = B G D♭ F

G7#5 = G B D# F

G13 = G B D E

ILLUSTRATION 6

1	2	3	4	5	6	7	8
G	A	B	C	D	E	F#	G

In this type of altered chord, the tonal movement takes place on the second string where 5th of the chord triad is located.

171

JAZZ CHORDS

ROOT IN BASS

3RD IN BASS

5TH IN BASS

OTHER CHORD FINGERINGS

JAZZ CHORDS

JAZZ CHORDS

JAZZ CHORDS

JAZZ CHORDS WITH CHROMATIC TONAL MOVEMENT

The term CHROMATIC TONAL MOVEMENT implies a succession of tones moving in Half Steps (one fret).

In the following chord forms the basic triad remains in one position while the EXTENSION, or ALTERATION, takes place on ONE STRING, usually moving in Half Steps, changing the chord TYPE by adding the MAJOR SEVENTH, DOMINANT SEVENTH, SIXTH, etc.

In this study of Jazz chords we will divide the more commonly used Jazz chords into three forms: the ROOT in the Bass, the THIRD in the Bass, and the FIFTH in the Bass, referring to the first, third, fifth notes of the Major Diatonic Scale that form the chord triad.

These advanced chord forms, using no open strings, are "movable", they may be played at each fret up and down the neck. To eliminate confusion and to aid the student in learning all of the altered and extended chords that may be developed from each chord form, they have been grouped by both fingering position, and chromatic tonal movement.

A definite program of learning should be applied to each form. Not only must a muscular memory pattern be developed to allow a smooth chord change through each series of chords, the student should also develop a complete understanding of how each chord is constructed. Learn what each position change means as you play each chord.

Each chord form represents only ONE chord, altered and extended to achieve all the possible chord types presented. Learn all of the chords by position and name at one fret, as shown in the Illustrations. Then learn what the names are as you progress up the neck. Each chord form can be moved twelve frets providing twelve basic chords plus all the altered and extended chords. All of these chords move chromatically on the 6th string.

FORM ONE — JAZZ CHORDS WITH THE ROOT IN THE BASS

In this chord form the root note is on the 6th string. To determine the chord's letter name— G, A, B♭, C, etc., use the six string Chromatic Scale. Example: If these four chords were played at the fifth fret, they would become A type chords as A is the correct note of the sixth string at the fifth fret.

Illustration One, the G Diatonic Scale, with the Root, third, fifth notes shown below, also has the three EXTENDED notes that are added to the three tone triad, the seventh, flatted seventh, and the sixth tones. These three additional tones, all one half step (one fret) apart, make up the three additional chords: G7, Gmaj7, G6.

FINGERING POSITIONS   ILLUSTRATION TWO

These four chords are played with the Root tone G on the sixth string, the BASS of the chord. The fifth and third of the chord remain on the same strings while the Chromatic Tonal Movement takes place on the fourth string. Observe the muted fifth and first strings. This is typical of Jazz chords which usually will be three or four tone chords.

MUSICAL NOTATION   ILLUSTRATION THREE

Here the tonal movement can be observed as it progresses down the staff from the Octave note, in the G chord, to the sixth tone in the G6 chord.

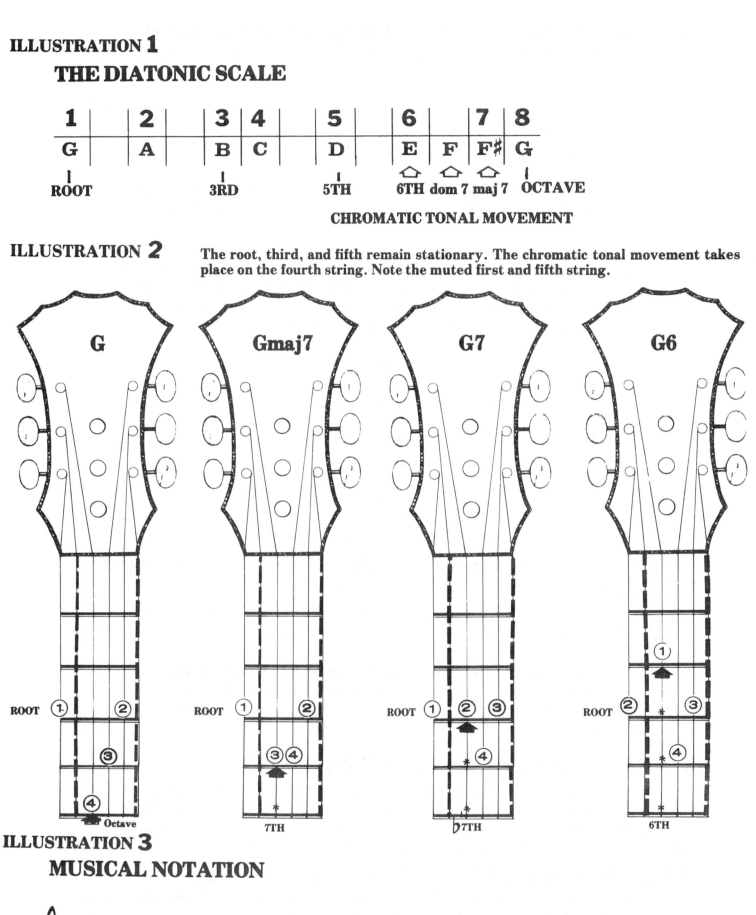

ROOT IN THE BASS

ILLUSTRATION 1
THE DIATONIC SCALE

1	2	3	4	5	6	7	8
G	A	B	C	D	E	F	F♯	G

ROOT   3RD   5TH   6TH   dom 7   maj 7   OCTAVE

CHROMATIC TONAL MOVEMENT

ILLUSTRATION 2

The root, third, and fifth remain stationary. The chromatic tonal movement takes place on the fourth string. Note the muted first and fifth string.

G   Gmaj7   G7   G6

ILLUSTRATION 3
MUSICAL NOTATION

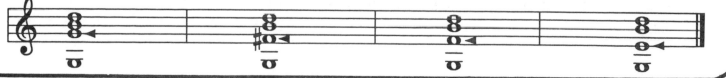

EIGHT ADDITIONAL G TYPE CHORDS

These eight additional *G* type chords are extensions or alterations of the basic *G* chord Root in Bass, studied on the previous page. Excluding the *Gdim7*, *Gaug*, and the *Gsus* chords, the three lower tones of the chord, the notes *G*—sixth string, *F*—fourth string, and *B*—third string, do not move. All tonal movement takes place on the second string.

GROUP ASSOCIATION THE EASIEST WAY TO LEARN

The student should develop the ability to play all of the "Root in the Bass" type chords. To facilitate learning this many chords, divide them into groups of generally the same chord type.

Learn the four chords—*G*, *Gmaj7*, *G7*, *G6* as a group, then learn the *G7♭5*, *G7+5*, *G7+5♭9* and the *G13* as another group. Then the three chords *G7sus*, *Gdim*, *Gaug* as a group. Learning by group association will help you understand the tonal movement of each group and give you a better understanding of how each chord is theoretically formed.

Watch for finger positions that are common to more than one chord, as in several chords, such as the *G7* and *G6*, the third and fourth fingers can be held in place while the first and second fingers are moved to change chords. This technique can be applied to many of the chords.

G7 ♭5   G7+5

Chord formula for *G7♭5*; R 3 ♭5 ♭7
$\qquad$ *G7+5*; R 3 +5 ♭7
These two chords are *G7*, Root in the Bass, chords with the tonal movement, the fifth, on the second string. Actually they are altered *G7* chords. Practice them as a group; *G7*, *G7♭5*, *G7+5*.

G9+5   G7 +5♭9

Chord formula for *G9+5*; R 3 +5 ♭7 9
$\qquad$ *G7+5♭9*; R 3 +5 ♭7 ♭9
These two chords are Dominant type chords and actually are the same chord, a *G7* with the ninth added. The seventh symbol is eliminated when writing the ninth, however when the ninth is altered as in the *G7+5♭9* we show the seventh symbol. The *G9+5* has a raised fifth while in the *G7+5♭9* we have the raised fifth and a lowered ninth.

G13

Chord formula for the *G13*; R 3 5 ♭7 9 13
This is a Dominant chord EXTENDED by adding the flatted seventh, ninth, and thirteenth note to the chord triad. The *G13* chord may be used as a direct substitute for the Dominant seventh chord. Example the *G13* for *G7*.

G7sus

Chord formula for *G7sus*; R 4 5 ♭7
This is a *G7* chord with the third raised one half step (one fret).

Gdim7

Chord formula for *G7sus*; R ♭3 ♭5 ♭7
This is an altered chord with the flatted seventh note added to the altered triad.

Gaug

Chord formula; R 3 #5
The *Gaug* is a *G* type chord with the fifth raised one half step (one fret).

ROOT IN THE BASS
EIGHT ADDITIONAL CHORDS

FINGERING POSITION

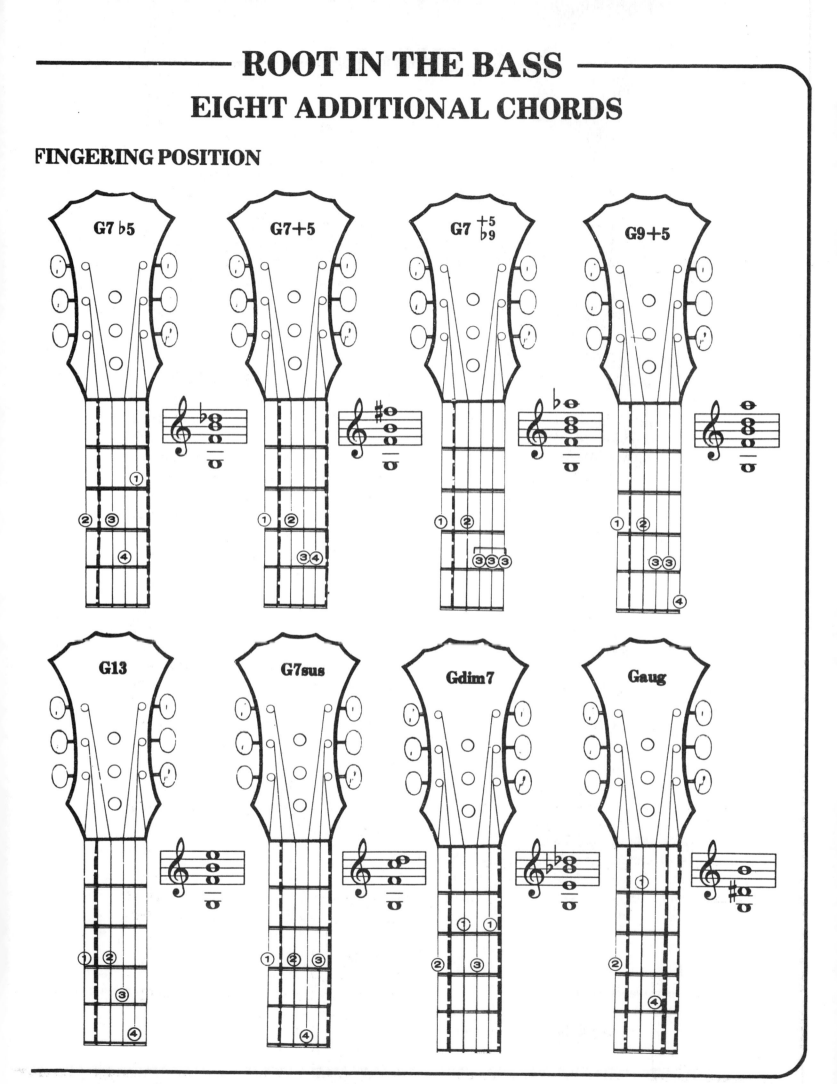

SIX ADDITIONAL CHORDS

These six chords complete this series of chords "With the Root In The Bass". These eighteen chords should be thoroughly studied and the ability to play them carefully developed. Since they are "movable" and can be played at least ten frets on any guitar, and twelve frets on a "Cut-away" model, you will be able to play a minimum of 180 Jazz chords with this chord form alone.

MINOR CHORDS WITH THE ROOT IN THE BASS

Gm6
Chord formula for *Gmi6*; R ♭3 5 6.
This is a *G* Major sixth with the third lowered.

Gm7
Chord formula for *Gmi7*; R ♭3 5 ♭7.
This is a Dominant seventh chord with the third lowered.

Gm9
Chord formula for *Gmi9*; R ♭3 5 ♭7 9.

Gm11
Chord formula; R ♭3 5 ♭7 11.
This is a Dominant Minor chord, flatted third, flatted seventh with the eleventh added.

G11
Chord formula; R 3 5 ♭7 9 11.
This is a Dominant chord, flatted seventh, with the ninth and eleventh added. In this chord form the third and fifth have been omitted. This is proper chord voicing with extended chords.

G+11
Chord formula; R 3 5 ♭7 9 +11
This is the Dominant chord, flatted seventh, with the eleventh raised one half step (one fret).

ROOT IN THE BASS
SIX ADDITIONAL CHORDS

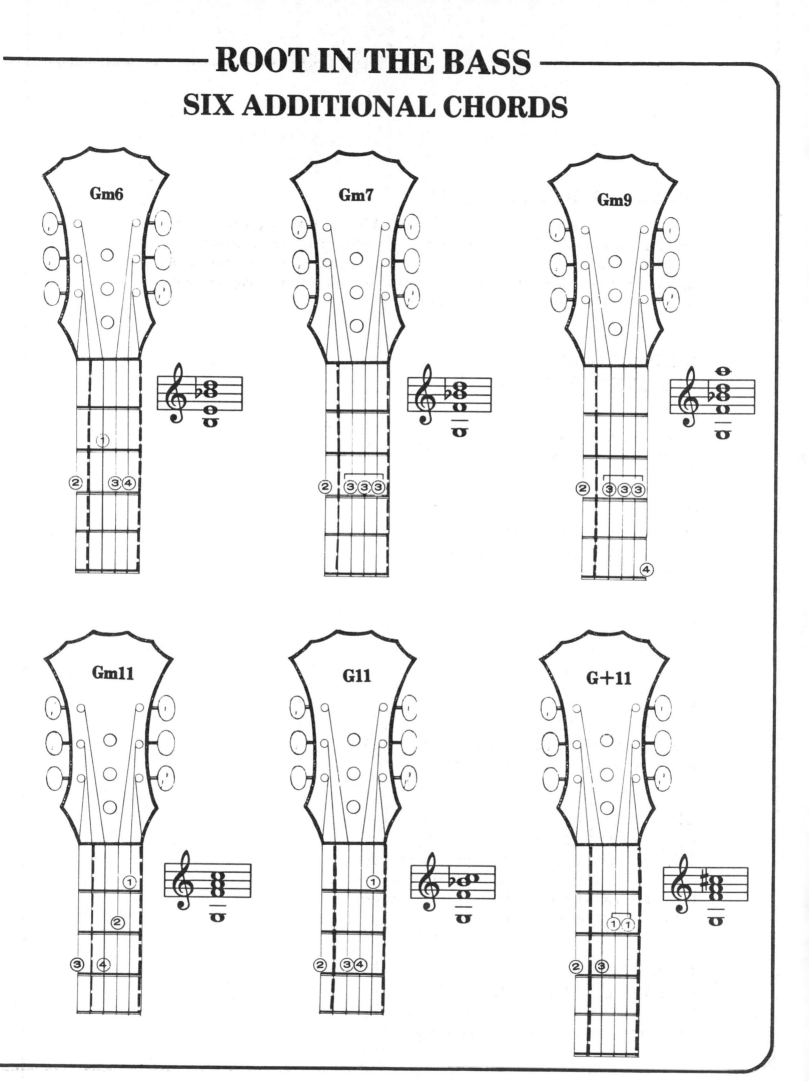

FORM TWO— JAZZ CHORDS WITH THE THIRD IN THE BASS—6TH STRING

These are all MOVABLE chords, no open strings, and progress up the neck Chromatically. *E♭* is the lowest position this chord form can be played in. Moved up one fret, these chords become *E* type chords. Move them up four frets and they are *G* type chords. In this chord form the Root tone is on the FOURTH string, and the chord name follows the fourth string Chromatic Scale.

MOVABLE CHORD FORMS

These four chords are played with the Root tone on the Fourth string, Illustration Two, the third on the sixth string, and the fifth on the third string. The Chromatic tonal movement takes place on the second string, progressing from the OCTAVE down the the MAJOR 7, down to the DOMINANT 7, and then to the SIXTH tone. The fifth and first strings are muted.

CHORD FORMULAS

E♭
Chord formula; R 3 5

E♭ maj7
Chord formula; R 3 5 7

E♭ 7
Chord formula; R 3 5 ♭7

E♭ 6
Chord formula; R 3 5 6

THIRD IN THE BASS

ILLUSTRATION 1

E♭ DIATONIC SCALE

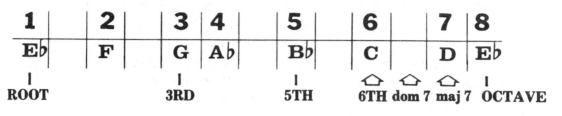

1	2	3	4	5	6		7	8
E♭	F	G	A♭	B♭	C		D	E♭
ROOT		3RD		5TH	6TH dom 7	maj 7		OCTAVE

CHROMATIC TONAL MOVEMENT

ILLUSTRATION 2

FINGERING POSITION

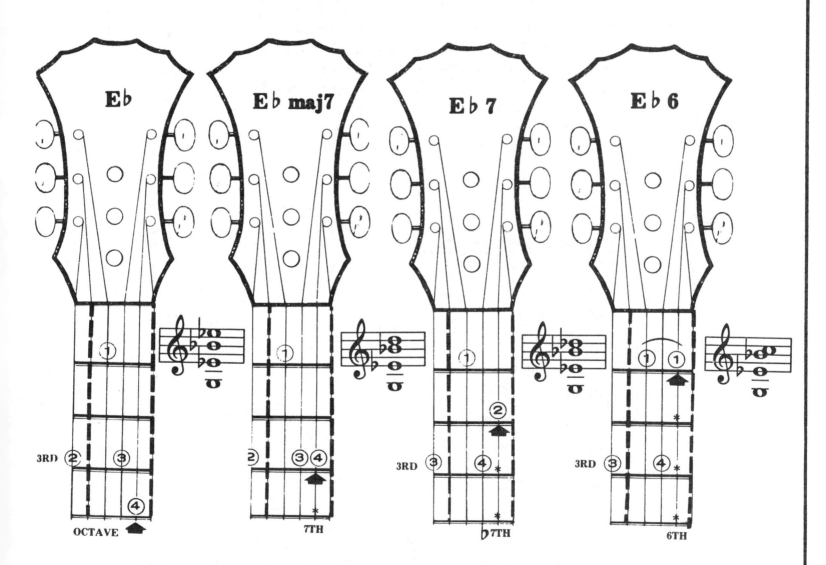

The root, third, and fifth remain stationary. The chromatic tonal movement occurs on the second string, moving in half steps, one fret at a time. NOTE: The first and fifth strings are muted.

MINOR CHORDS WITH THE THIRD IN THE BASS

These four Minor chords with the 3rd of the triad in the bass completes this chord form.

Actually they are not different chords from those shown on the previous page, the Major chords.

By lowering the third, located on the sixth string, the Major chord becomes a MINOR chord. The fingerings required to make the three chords, MAJOR 7, DOMINANT 7, and the SIXTH chords are the same as the three MAJOR type chords simplifying the learning process as you need only learn four chord types.

FINGERING POSITIONS

Illustration One shows the fingering positions required to play these four MINOR chords.

MUSICAL NOTATION

Illustration Two shows the musical notation of each chord as they appear in written form.

CHORD FORMULAS

E♭ mi
Chord formula; R ♭3 5

E♭ mi maj7
Chord formula; R ♭3 5 7

E♭ mi7
Chord formula; R ♭3 5 ♭7

E♭ mi6
Chord formula; R ♭3 5 6

MINOR CHORDS

ILLUSTRATION 1

FINGERING POSITIONS

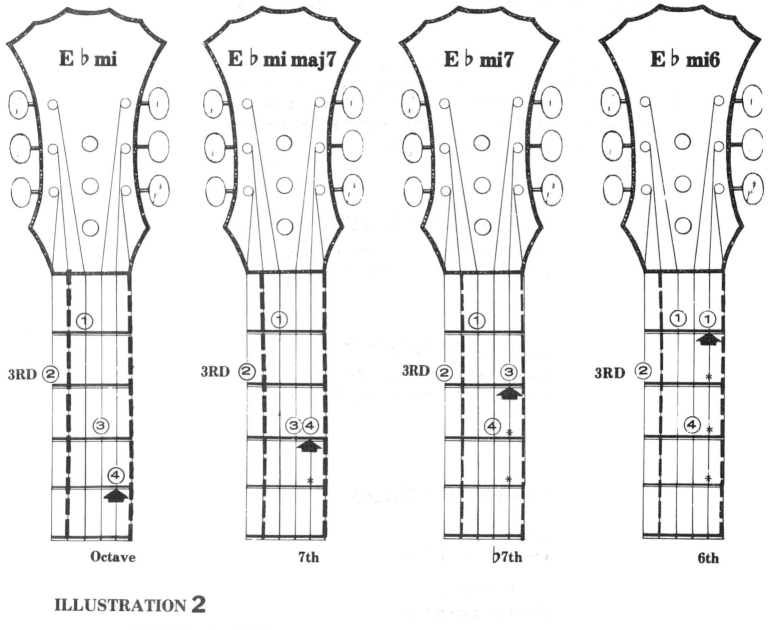

E♭ mi	E♭ mi maj7	E♭ mi7	E♭ mi6
Octave	7th	♭7th	6th

ILLUSTRATION 2

MUSICAL NOTATION

E♭ mi E♭ mi maj7 E♭ mi7 E♭ mi6

183

FORM THREE—JAZZ CHORDS WITH THE FIFTH IN THE BASS

The DIATONIC SCALE, Illustration One, with the Root, third, and fifth notes shown below it, also has the three "extended" notes that may be added to the three tone triad—the seventh, flatted seventh, and the sixth note. These three additional notes, all one half step apart (one fret), make up the three additional chords—*C*, *Cmaj7*, *C7*, and *C6*.

FINGERING POSITION

These four chords are played with the FIFTH tone on the sixth string, Illustration Two. The third is on the fourth string. The Root tone is omitted in this chord form. Since the Fifth is on the sixth string and the Root omitted, the six string Chromatic Scale is used to determine the chord name. For example, the note *G*, sixth string is the fifth of the *C* chord, move this chord form up to the fifth fret and the sixth string note is *A*, the fifth of the chord *D*. The Chromatic tonal movement takes place on the third string, progressing from the octave down to the Major 7, down to the Dominant 7, and then to te Sixth tone. The first and second tones are muted.

MUSICAL NOTATION

Illustration Three shows the musical notation of these four chords as they appear written on the musical staff.

CHORD FORMULAS

C
Chord formula; R 3 5

Cmaj7
Chord formula; R 3 5 7

C7
Chord formula; R 3 5 $\flat$7

C6
Chord formula; R 3 5 6

FIFTH IN THE BASS

ILLUSTRATION **1**

C DIATONIC SCALE

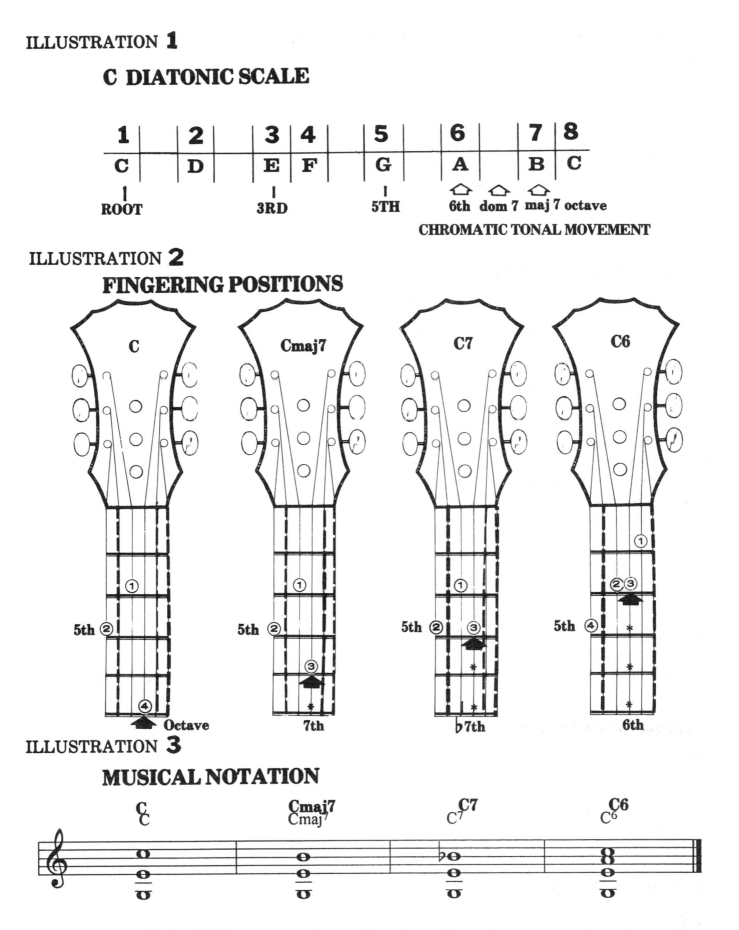

The third and fifth remain stationary. The chromatic tonal movement takes place
on the third string, moving in half steps, one fret at a time. Note the muted first,
second, and fifth strings.

These are all MOVABLE chords, no open strings and progress up the neck Chromatically. C♯ (B) is the lowest position this chord form can be played in. Move up two frets and this chord form will be *D* type chords.

C7+5 C7♭5

Chord formula for *C7+5;* R 3 #5 ♭7
C7♭5; R 3 ♭5 ♭7
These two chords are both *C7*, fifth in the bass, with the tonal movement on the sixth string. Actually they are altered *C7* chords. Practice them as a group—*C7*, *C7+5*, *C7♭5*, etc.

C9 C7+9 C7♭9

Chord formula for *C9;*   R 3 5 ♭7 9
C7+9; R 3 5 ♭7 +9
C7♭9; R 3 5 ♭7 ♭9
These three chords are Dominant type chords as they have the flatted seventh and the ninth added to the chord triad. The seventh symbol is omitted when writing a *C9*. It is used when we alter the chord.

Cmaj9

Chord formula for *Cmaj9;* R 3 5 ♭7 9 13
This is a *C* Major chord with the ninth note added to the chord. This is an EXTENDED chord as the ninth note (*D*), is actually a third interval above the *Cmaj7.*

C13

Chord formula for *C13;* R 3 5 ♭7 9 13
This is a Dominant chord EXTENDED by adding the flatted seventh, ninth, and thirteenth notes to the chord triad. The Dominant thirteenth chord may be used in direct substitution for the Dominant seven chord (*C13* for *C7*).

C13♭9

Chord formula for *C13♭9;* R 3 5 ♭7 ♭9 13
This chord form is an ALTERED Dominant thirteen chord. As shown, the ninth has been lowered one fret, flatting the ninth of the chord.

C6 add 9

Chord formula for *C6add9;* R 3 5 6 9
This is a Major sixth chord with the ninth added. This is a direct substitution chord for any MAJOR type chord, and can be used exceptionally well in place of the Major sixth chord. The ninth is often added to the Major sixth chord. The chord form shown here is derived from the Major sixth with the fifth in the bass. When practicing this chord, associate it with the *C6* chord. NOTE: The Root tone had been eliminated when the ninth was added.

C7sus

Chord formula for the *C7sus;* R 4 5 ♭7
This is a Dominant chord with the third of the triad raised one fret. The suspension is a non-chordal tone and creates added interest by delaying the normally expected chord tone.

FIFTH IN THE BASS

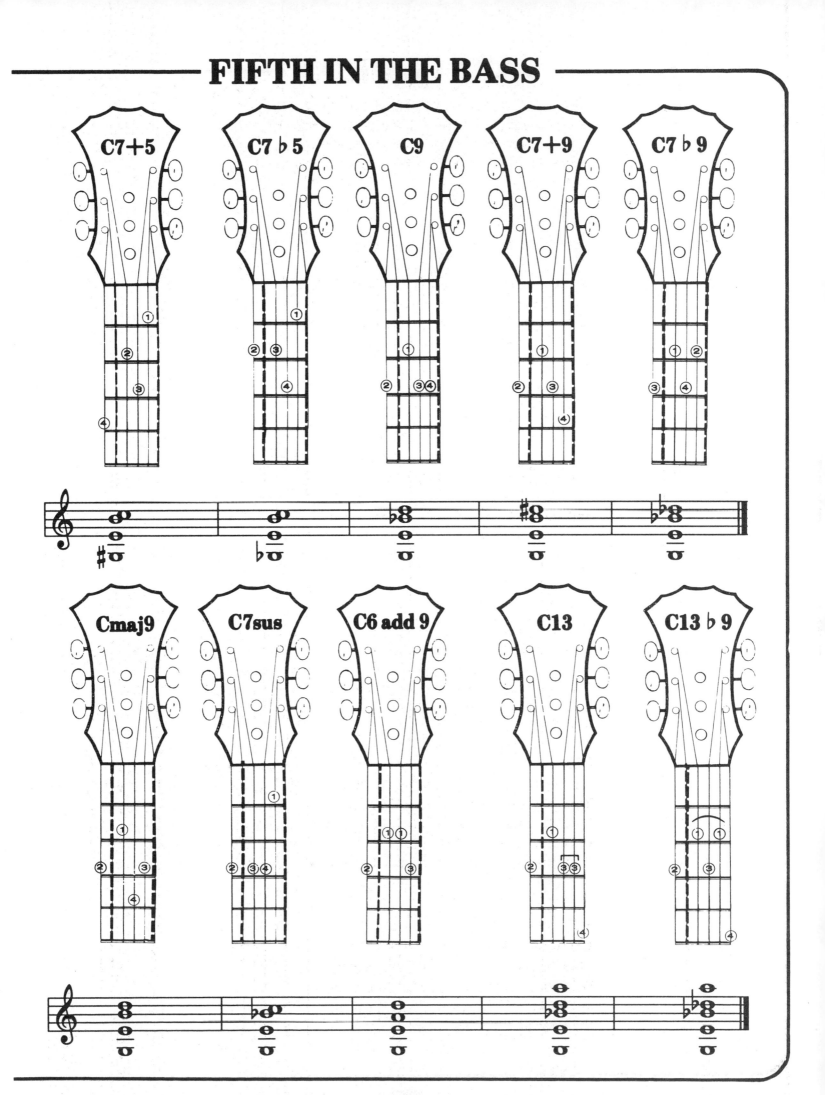

MINORS
FIFTH IN THE BASS

Study these Minor chords as a group as they are actually one chord ALTERED, or EXTENDED to build the chord forms shown.

Cmi

Chord formula for *Cmi*; R ♭3 5
The Minor chord is built by lowering the third of the chord triad one fret (a half step).

Cmi7

Chord formula for the *Cmi7*; R ♭3 5 ♭7
This is a Dominant seven chord. All tonal movement takes place on the fourth string.

Cmi6

The chord formula for the *Cmi6*; R ♭3 5 6
This is a Minor chord with the sixth note added.

Cmi7♭5

Chord formula for the *Cmi7 5*; R ♭3 ♭5♭7
This is a Minor seven with the fifth lowered.

FIFTH IN THE BASS
MINOR CHORDS

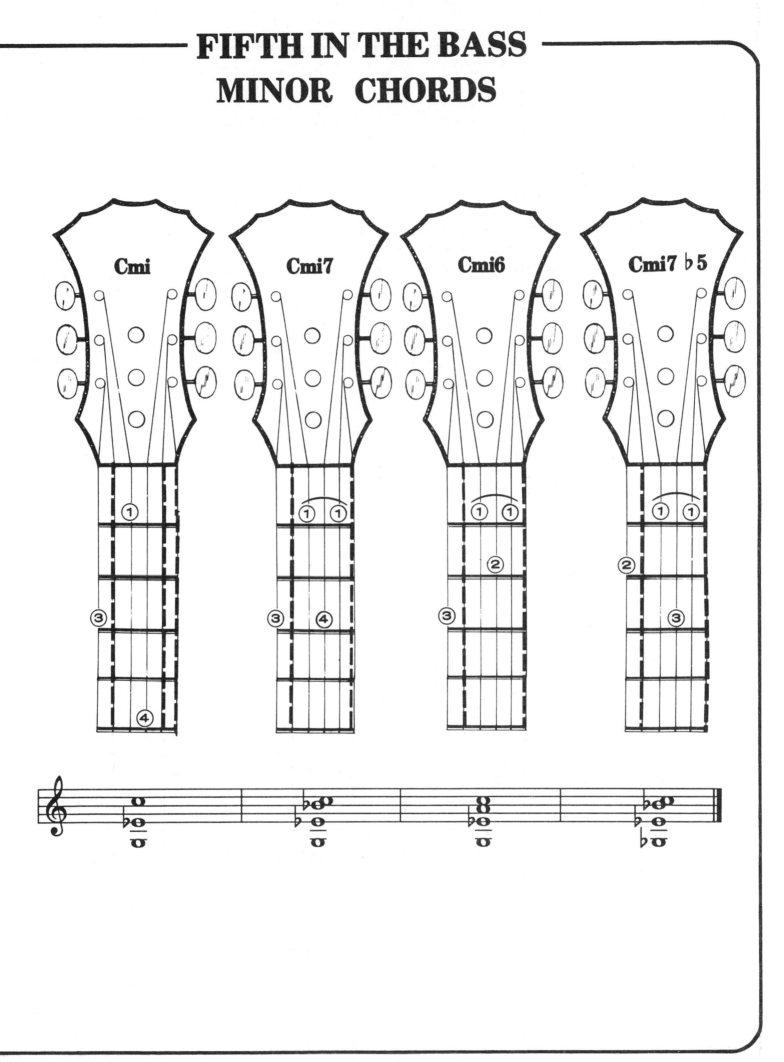

ALPHABETICAL CHORD LISTING

CROSS REFERENCE INDEX

To Learn··Teach